Finding Your Kingdom Sweet Spot

A Spiritual Handbook for High Impact Entrepreneurs

EXPANDED EDITION

John R. Bost

ISBN 979-8-88644-389-9 (Paperback)
ISBN 979-8-88644-390-5 (Digital)

Covenant Books
11661 Hwy 707
Murrells Inlet, SC 29576
www.covenantbooks.com

For my grandchildren, John Luther and Caroline Elizabeth,
as a playbook for their young lives.
Perhaps long after I have departed, they will find
wisdom for their various endeavors.

ENDORSEMENTS

"*Finding Your Kingdom Sweet Spot* is a powerful guide for the young aspiring entrepreneur who desires to glorify God in the marketplace. It's rare to have an opportunity to be mentored by a catalytic business leader with such rich cross-sector experience as John Bost has, and that is the gift found within these pages."

Shae Bynes, Author, *Grace Over Grind*
Founder of Kingdom Driven Entrepreneur

"In this latest work, John continues challenging us to reconsider the ways we interpret the message and divine nature of Christ. Through his own marketplace experiences, John shines light on our historically narrow understanding of the scope of Christ's teachings while inviting us to a deeper, more expansive understanding of who we are in Christ Jesus as well as who He truly was and is. This book is for anyone seeking a more authentic understanding of Christ's invitation to unpack their personal calling."

Steve Gallagher, Executive Coach
Associate Dean of Students
University of North Carolina School of the Arts

"The messages are great, the lessons learned are thought-provoking, and I will pray that you touch the lives of many people with your message of His Gospel embedded in the words of your thesis!"

Tim Bertram
CEO, ProKidney

"John's prophetic heart and perspective offers people of faith a true hope. For those deeply wanting to impact their faith, family, and community, John provides thoughtful questions to explore. His perspective on history, faith, philanthropy, and entrepreneurial living is a treasure of honesty, humility, and hope. A worthy read for sure!"

Eddie Hammett, Author
Master Certified Coach
Leadership & Life Transitions Coach

"As a person who has been mentored by John in my early pastoral days and thereafter, I've always been inspired by his vision for the kingdom and the strategic way he follows the heart of God. What he has written in the pages of *Finding Your Kingdom Sweet Spot* is exactly what I have witnessed in my twenty-three years of knowing him. He walks the walk. As a missionary to the community, John's God-inspired wisdom in these pages and throughout his life have been life changing for me. His sharing of his journey to his kingdom sweet spot in these pages informs, inspires, directs, and affirms our own kingdom calling. Delve into it and glean from his wisdom. You will go deeper, and you will be changed!"

Michele Powell, MS, CRC
Author, *15 Minutes of Unpacking Our Grief*
Leadership Development Speaker/Trainer
Diversity Advocate

"I read two thirds of *Finding Your Kingdom Sweet Spot* in one reading because I couldn't put it down. John Bost is a longtime friend and entrepreneur who lives and walks by Kingdom principles. As a retired Literacy Specialist, I find his book to be a valuable guide for *all* Christ followers, whatever your calling may be. Here's to living out your anointing, making an impact upon your community, and finding your Kingdom sweet spot!"

De Harvey Ewing, Literacy Specialist

"*Finding Your Kingdom Sweet Spot* by John Bost is a simple but robust read. While many people simply live a life learning the 'hows', John's writing takes you not only 'how' but also to the 'why', which is the most important question to answer for your life calling and identity. John is not just a theorist but also a practitioner. This book helps you to obtain clarity and next steps and reminds me of the wisdom in 1 Corinthians 15:58: 'Therefore, my dear brothers and sisters, stand firm. Let nothing move you. Always give yourselves fully to the work of the Lord, because you know that your labor in the Lord is not in vain.' I am grateful for John and his thoughts placed into writing. Thank you, John, for sharing yourself with others."

Rick Hughes
Consultant*Coach*Crisis Response Specialist
Revitalization Consultant & Coach
Certified Life-Younique Coach

"Bost is at his best in *Finding Your Kingdom Sweet Spot*. He reminds readers that life isn't about what you do but who you are; Not about finding your "calling" but following Christ; not about the work you're in but your walk through life; not about your profession but the person you are becoming in Christ. Bost puts it like this: 'The more you understand yourself in relation to God, the better you'll understand that your calling has little to do with you and everything to do with Him.' So, if you're looking for a relationship with God or what it is God may be calling you to do in life, you're reading a biblical and practical guide from one who has discovered the sublime secret to a fulfilling life. And that secret is really no secret at all—simply, you are innately equipped to live a God-called, God-connected, and uniquely-creative life. By making God your life ambition, your calling will emerge much more naturally as you curiously explore the innate gifts and interests with which God has endowed you. This is how to find and follow your 'Kingdom Sweet Spot.'"

Dr. Steve McSwain
President and CEO at Foundation
for Excellence in Giving, Inc.
"Thought Leader in Spirituality & Generosity"

Two things make *Finding Your Kingdom Sweet Spot* an outstanding book. First, is that John Bost wrote it. If you knew John like I know John, you would discover a person who is a personification of finding his sweet spot and following God into the marketplace as a high impact entrepreneur. Second, I celebrate several themes essential for high impact Christ-centered entrepreneurs -- recognition of God's call on your life, understanding how God has gifted you spiritually and strategically, serving people with compassionate values, and being captivated by great passion for God's Kingdom.

George Bullard
Strategic Thinking Mentor
ForthTelling Innovation

CONTENTS

FOREWORD

I play golf.

I am still not sure why I love a game that is so hard. Some wit has noted that golf spelled backward is flog. Golfers, too, often leave the course feeling flayed because the game punishes poor shots more than most sports. In basketball, if you shoot an air ball or rim out a layup—no big deal—a bucket is only worth a couple points (and you only make about 40 percent of them anyway). Not so in golf. In golf, strike an errant tee shot or two, and you're going to feel flogged. The reason that amateur golfers' shots wind up in tall weeds, thick forests, and deep lakes so often is that the face of the club isn't very big, and most weekend hackers don't have the balance and mechanics to hit the ball consistently on the middle of such a small clubface.

But every now and then, a golfer finds it!

It feels delicious and delightful. The ball flies straight and strong. It makes the golfer come back next time, searching for one more shot—in the sweet spot.

That's the gift John Bost has for you in the pages ahead—visionary help in finding your sweet spot, not in golf, but in your life.

John Bost's eighth-grade teacher once was overheard speaking about her middle school student: "Why don't you ask Johnny for his ideas? He always has great ideas!" He still does. But in the pages ahead, you're not just invited to hear John's ideas—you're invited to listen for God's ideas. There is more here than sound counsel for business innovators—there is spiritual revelation for the thirsty!

Finding your Kingdom sweet spot is no mere intellectual exercise for the thinkers, nor is it luck that befalls the fortunate. What John Bost describes in the pages ahead is vocation, like the root of the word: voice. There's a divine voice mixed into these chapters and an invitation to let God's promptings meld with your "gut" longings. It's puzzling that wisdom comes as late in the game as it does, but usually it does. His savvy has not come cheap; it has been forged in the fires of entrepreneurial trials and triumphs. When I accepted a call to serve a local congregation in Winston-Salem two and a half decades ago, I found in John a partner who dreamed of a Kingdom-kissed community—a changed city. He hasn't stopped dreaming. He hasn't stopped working.

Most novice golfers are tempted to just swing harder in a desperate effort to make the ball go farther. But more experienced golfers discover a secret—it's better to swing slow and hit the ball in the sweet spot. The sweet spot makes everything go farther. John Bost has found his sweet spot, and he's inspiring to be around. I love his big vision, his big heart, and his big faith. If you don't yet know him, read ahead—you'll love him, too.

Alan D. Wright, Author, *The Power to Bless*
Senior Pastor, Reynolda Presbyterian,
Winston-Salem, NC
Pastoralan.org

INTRODUCTION

For most of us, the majority of our waking hours are spent at work. Yet many times there is a disconnect between Sunday morning and the rest of the week. Many see work as an aspect of their life unrelated to their spiritual self, or simply a means to fund ministry and other life pursuits. For active leaders the work week is so demanding—on top of commitments to family and friends—that the prospect of having a "real ministry" (as traditionally defined) is seen as an unscalable wall. As a result, our gifted leaders can become frustrated and disengaged from the ministry. Their participation is diminished to attending services, a few years on the board, and an occasional missions project. All these are important contributions, but the Body of Christ, one's community, and even the individual are often robbed of their potential for greatness.

Christian service should not be limited to the mission field, soup kitchens, or activities within the walls of the church. It should also occur in boardrooms, classrooms, civil service, etc., where believers spend most of their lives. True success in this life requires movement beyond an internal focus on our relationship with God and toward passionately pursuing our external call to serve humanity. A significant challenge for the church is to help members understand how Kingdom principles apply to the uncharted waters of the marketplace, to focus on their occupations as ministry, and to use secular positions (if there is such a thing) as a forum for gifts and talents to create significant opportunity to serve God by serving community.

Work as a ministry has maybe never crossed the minds of some people who think that their role in the body of Christ is to fund those who do ministry or be a mere observer of it. The reality is every single person is uniquely called to represent Jesus in the different environments of their lives. It doesn't have to be full-time ministry *or* a career as an entrepreneur; it should be full-time ministry *as* an entrepreneur. We can express our spirit-given gifts and talents in the marketplace and thereby represent God to the people around us who need hope the most.

When our lives as entrepreneurs are integrated with our spiritual selves, that's when we have true impact in our communities. That is when we've found our Kingdom sweet spot. The term sweet spot is quite old and, in fact, very diverse in original usage. Athletically, it's the place on a piece of sports equipment that provides maximum speed and control. I have most often thought of the term sweet spot relative to leadership theory and of late, when one experiences those sudden holy and joyful moments when vocation and spiritual impact most align.

The sweet spot in your entrepreneurial career is when you are using your gifts, pursuing your passions, honoring your values, and serving your community with the work that you're doing. Finding your Kingdom sweet spot, as Christ followers, means that the work you're doing and how you approach your work is reflective of the Kingdom of God.

We are all capable of finding our Kingdom sweet spot. Though certain psychological inventories and the like may add professional inputs for shaping our careers, there are no tests that need to be taken, no qualifications or certifications that need to be acquired for you to begin your journey; you are already Kingdom qualified as you are today. The question is, are you ready to engage in Kingdom business? The engaged, Kingdom-qualified leader changes the lives of the individuals they encounter daily and in turn, has a greater impact through their business or industry, upon our economy, their country, and the world.

As I age and reflect on the life experience gained during my fifty years as a devoted church leader, entrepreneur at heart, and hard worker in multiple business and municipal sectors, I am trying to decipher my blessed life, its purpose, and how best to use these last few years for God's glory. My wife has watched me now for fifty years wrestle with a calling to our local community, the Village of

Clemmons and my nearby hometown of Winston-Salem, North Carolina. It has taken different forms over the years and led me into five different sectors, but the call remains the same: to be the hands and feet of Jesus in my city. I determined to live my life fully dependent upon the empowerment and provision of the Lord—unbounded by circumstance and systems.

I am always encouraged by the words from Jeremiah, for it was this ancient book that shifted my profession, first from education to pastoral ministry, and finally to the marketplace, "Wherever I send you seek that city, if not this one, the next. I'll give you a city" (Jeremiah 29:7 paraphrased). Words from the Lord that have compelled my matriculation through these various sectors of community service.

I started my career as an educator, teaching high schoolers chemistry straight out of college. I loved being a teacher and what I expected to be a two-year gig to help me pay off debt turned into over thirty years of passionate commitment to the education of the youths in nearby schools, both public and private. After fifteen years in the classroom, I was encouraged to pursue a degree in community education. With that also came a certification in resource development.

Immediately thereafter, a position opened in administration with the Lexington City Schools, which then led to an Education Specialist Degree (Ed.S.) in leadership and administration, along with a superintendent's certification.

While in the education sector, I was also very involved in my church, leading prayer breakfasts and teaching Bible studies. My knowledge of foundations, along with an appointment to serve at the state and national level in our church denomination, led to an opportunity to serve as executive pastor in a local church followed by a couple of ordinations.

By the mid-nineties, I had launched my own for-profit consulting firm, Master Counsel & Associates, Inc, assuming that I might be of benefit to the institutional church and the community in general, given the focus of my degrees in leadership and resource development, tenure in public education, nonprofit engagement, and my executive pastor role in a rather large congregation. My broad experience seemed sufficient platform to step out upon.

I have spent the last twenty years in community development in some capacity. I served seven years on the Winston-Salem/Forsyth County Planning Board, was a part of various Early Childhood initiatives; I served as Chairman of Leadership Winston-Salem; and served three terms as the Mayor of Clemmons, North Carolina. Throughout my years in five different sectors, I've seen God move in big and small ways. And throughout that array of opportunities, He's invited me to be a part of bringing His Kingdom to my city and community.

My wife and I have been unbelievably favored and blessed with relational capital over the years and with that, a measure of financial success. All my different life-long continuing education endeavors now reveal a seamless Kingdom strategy. One that I could not possibly have known in my early days teaching the sciences. I can truly say that Divine providence, and the calling now followed have surely made a way for me, even before I had yet chosen the path. From an aloof first-generation college student, now with three advanced degrees, and four other books in print, there still seemed one story yet unwritten, longing to be told.

In this book, I want to share the practices I've used to build God's Kingdom in the different sectors over the course of my career and life. To some, my story might sound a little like that of a restless wanderer, but to me, it has been a rich journey and appropriate preparation for this very moment, with my desire being to become the mentor that I never had. With an exit ramp in sight, howbeit to a joyous destination, I hope to leave behind lessons learned during my seventy-four-year entrepreneurial journey.

To grow as an entrepreneur and Christ follower, focusing on your personal awareness, spiritual growth, and community development will be essential to finding your sweet spot. We cannot cleanly separate the personal, spiritual, and relational aspects of our lives. They are all entwined and inextricably connected. Growing in each of these areas means becoming more of who you were created to be in God's image. By examining each of these three areas and how they relate to one another, constituting a whole person and a much fuller life, we can find our Kingdom sweet spots and discover how these areas help us become high-impact entrepreneurs for the Kingdom of God.

I trust this book, within its margins, along with end of chapter inquiries and blank lines provided, can serve as a handbook for budding entrepreneurs. Make these pages a sacred journal, a place to capture God-thoughts that, when implemented, will serve generations to come. As you progress through the various stages of becoming an entrepreneur, I trust you will find yourself doing the Kingdom's business, rather than simply a Christian doing business. Entrepreneurs, such as yourself, may just become God's new evangelists, with a more promising future than you might have felt in these last few years in America. It is my prayerful sense that the next transformational moment in America will emerge from among the current explosion of entrepreneurs, millennials, and beyond, many seeking a new model for the institutional church as we know it.

Just as John the Baptist prepared the way for Jesus coming to the earth, I pray that the entrepreneurs of today will prepare the way for the Kingdom of God:

> The voice of one calling: "In the wilderness prepare the way for the Lord; make straight in the desert a highway for our God. Every valley shall be raised up, every mountain and hill made low; the rough ground shall become level, the rugged places a plain. And the glory of the Lord will be revealed, and all people will see it together. For the mouth of the Lord has spoken." (Isaiah 40:3–5)

My calling is making straight in a desert land, the highways upon which folk trod in the search for the God who is love. Every low place in the troubled world is raised up as I walk through it! That might sound arrogant, but it expresses the reality of one Spirit-filled and on point in their life's calling.

As I interact with others, my presence and giftings should make mountains more scalable, hills then become only bumps in the road, and the rugged places, well hey, been there done that! Take a hold of hope in a way that the glory of the Lord might be shown to those around you. Bring fresh wind, new possibilities to those around you today. The true Christ-follower offers more than pious words, rather practical solutions in the marketplace, laced with love.

The challenge being offered is for you to fully unpack the calling so uniquely assigned while sharing the insights and ideation that will be divinely revealed. The success you'll have in the Kingdom business will not be defined by any title or possession you attain, but rather by the love you share with those in your community and city. As you focus on **personal awareness, spiritual growth, and community development** (note Sweet Spot Diagram) in the coming chapters, you'll begin to uncover your Kingdom sweet spot, meanwhile carving a path for others to follow in your footsteps.

PART 1

Personal Awareness

CHAPTER 1

The Question of Calling

When you get your, "Who am I?", question right, all of your, 'What should I do?' questions tend to take care of themselves.
—Richard Rohr, *Falling Upward*

To truly be catalysts for God's Kingdom on earth, we need to look inward and build our personal awareness of who we are, of who God created us to be. When we look inward at our identities, passions, giftings, proclivities, fears, and uniqueness, it will allow us to deepen our relationship with God and better understand our roles in the marketplace as entrepreneurs and Kingdom catalysts.

I think we all struggle at some point in time with determining what our purpose on this earth is. How can we best use our gifts to make a difference on this earth in the limited time we have? I struggled with my calling for some years, and though I was quite successful in terms of my resume, both in the school system and while contributing to the growth of a megachurch campus, all along there was a deeper desire to fully understand the true concept of "full-time ministry." The context of a calling was still quite misunderstood and explaining a desire to "minister in the marketplace" back then seemed ahead of its time, though not for long. Today, it is common language to those who grasp the Kingdom of God as more than a church or an end-of-life destination.

Having now been self-employed for twenty-five years, I realize that one's vocation, regardless of theological alignment, is full-time ministry. "For the Kingdom of God is not meat and drink; but righteousness, peace and joy" (Romans 14:17 KJV). Those spiritual elements are found not in one's possessions, but in one's *vocàre*. The word *vocàre* is, to me, a verb implying a sovereign womb work accomplished long before birth, preparing one for their life's vocation and Kingdom impact. We experience righteousness, peace, and joy, only as we begin to walk into that "womb-work."

If I might paraphrase a recent statement from Pastor Alan Wright, *a calling is not an invitation; it's not something you might get around to later. A calling is a "before you were formed in your mother's womb" event, a foreordained kind of appointment, empowerment, and anointing. It is a God-appointed fit for your life, your human destiny, and eternity's plan. What I like to refer to as calling is a spiritual consecration; think set apart, yes and again, that womb-work, foreordained long before your birth. The "anointing," the hand of God upon your life, once fully surrendered, far exceeds any skills learned in life though they, too, are beneficial.*

I have learned, over my fifty years in the professional world, that calling is less about the work that you are doing and more about who you're doing it for. Your anointing follows you wherever you go, in whatever field you enter. I believe the Holy Spirit will help guide you, and your unique skill sets and passions will make paths clear to you, but regardless of where you are or what you end up doing, you are a light, an ordained child of God, anointed, and that can't be taken away from you.

Part of a Bigger Picture

When your calling becomes less centered on the field of work you go into, you can experience the true freedom of exploring different options and finding what feels right. I believe we are all called to help the people around us in whatever city and community we are in. The reality is, we are all part of the Kingdom business—building the Kingdom of God on earth so that more people may know and experience His love and grace. The role we play in bringing the Kingdom to earth matters less than our dedication to showing God's love to the people around us in our communities.

If we think about Jesus' ministry on earth, we realize it was very community driven. He went around helping people however He could, in whatever way they needed to be helped. And while our skill sets are seemingly more limited than this God-man Jesus, we need only to look at how He called His disciples. He didn't call them to a particular field or give them a particular responsibility, He just said "follow me." And He calls us to do the same. Jesus' disciples moved with Him. Wherever Jesus went, they followed. Whatever Jesus asked them to do, they did: feeding the community, healing people, casting out demons, and telling people the good news about Jesus.

Getting caught up in the question of what you are called to misses the main point. You have been called. Period. God wants you to make His name known and make His name great, and He will fill you in on all the details you need. All you need do is walk with Him, day in and day out, just like the disciples did. True intimacy with God, building a deep relationship with Him, is your big purpose in life, and as you do that, God will fill you in on ways to share that purpose with others.

As God said through His prophet Jeremiah, if your city prospers, you too will prosper (see Jeremiah 29:7). In our world today, many influential entrepreneurs have turned inward, hoarding money, while not paying the people who make that wealth possible a living wage. That is evil and cruel, and I believe that we are called to something greater. Making a god out of accruing wealth will ultimately lead to spiritual lack, a scarcity mindset, dissatisfaction, and loneliness. When leaders in the entrepreneurial world are more concerned about taking care of the people in their community and making sure the people around them are prospering, that is when they have the most long-lasting and tangible impact on this earth. That is the service we are called to as Christ followers, that is what we're aiming for.

The more you understand yourself in relation to God, the better you'll understand that your calling has little to do with you and everything to do with Him. Your identity, purpose, personality, and gifts are so inseparable from Him and His love for you, and the more you understand that the harder it becomes to separate Sunday from the rest of the week.

You do not need a background in theology or a doctorate in ministry to make a difference for God in your community. You just need to partner with God, meeting with Him daily; the rest is just following His lead. You already have your holy anointing; you now just have to live it out.

Kingdom Assignments

If you are already an entrepreneur or feel a bent toward that in your life, but aren't sure if it's what you are called to, I hope you realize the ways your life can be in "full-time ministry" no matter what field you are in. Just as our understanding of God unfolds and evolves throughout our lifetime, so too, I believe, does our particular Kingdom assignments. Even though I've explored five different sectors throughout the course of my career, I believe that every single job and sector prepared me for the next one. It wasn't that I was lost and trying to find my way, I think that each of those jobs were assignments from God that made His name known and prepared me for the next assignment He had for me.

Now, I'm not saying that God doesn't call us to more specific assignments, I believe He does. But grasping that we can't miss our calling because it is inherent within us gives us the foundation of freedom we need to listen to God more closely as we seek the Kingdom assignments He has given us.

In Philippians 1:3–6 Paul writes, "I thank my God every time I remember you. In all my prayers for all of you, I always pray with joy because of your partnership in the gospel from the first day until now, being confident of this, that he who began a good work in you will carry it on to completion until the day of Christ Jesus." God began a good work in you when you were "knit together in [your] mother's womb" (Psalm 139:13). And He will complete His good work in your life through your partnership in the gospel. Paul doesn't say exactly what this will look like since it is unique and different for everyone, but the purpose and drive is the same: partnering to share the gospel with others on this earth.

Whether you are decades into your career or trying to figure out what you're going to be when you "grow up," I hope this book will help you navigate your life path so that you can make a way for others who come after you to better support and provide for the people in their communities. I can tell you my journey has been quite different than my mind first envisioned when at the age of nine, I heard the voice that has since led my life say, "One day, you will preach the gospel." My preaching has been less from a pulpit and more in the marketplace as a "serial entrepreneur." Now I believe that's exactly what God had in mind.

How Well He Knows Us

I did not climb a ladder of worldly success; I instead took a divine path that has led me to many different places through which I attained a unique understanding of God, His people, and the world around me. Your journey will likewise be unique. I am humbly attempting to be quite transparent and trust the reader will sense that going forward. As I was writing this chapter, God shared this insight with me: "Allow the circumstances of your life to determine your certifications," in essence to guide your professional credentials, though God uniquely equips us for our Kingdom assignments. Whatever circumstances you've faced in your life are equipping you for how and where God will work through you for the benefit of people in your community. The sooner we accept and embrace that reality, the quicker we'll be able to be the hands and feet of Jesus in the way He intends for us to be.

God knows us better than anyone ever has or ever will. He knows us so intimately and has created us with specific gifts and passions to grow His Kingdom in unique ways. In Psalm 139:14–18, David writes about just how well God knows each one of His children:

> I praise you because I am fearfully and
> wonderfully made; your works are wonderful, I

know that full well. My frame was not hidden
from you when I was made in the secret place,
when I was woven together in the depths of the
earth. Your eyes saw my unformed body; all the
days ordained for me were written in your book
before one of them came to be. How precious
to me are your thoughts, God! How vast is the
sum of them! Were I to count them, they would
out-number the grains of sand—when I awake, I
am still with you.

God has uniquely made you, knows what each day of your life
will hold, and has plans and purposes for your life that you wouldn't
believe if He told you. He is preparing you for and equipping you
with everything you need to be a Kingdom catalyst in your community and find your specific sweet spot within the Kingdom.

I believe the next major transformational moment in the body
of Christ will come through the Christian entrepreneurs now being
raised up across the globe! As circumstances present themselves, one
should prayerfully discern if each might be a "word from the Lord."
Not all words are audible. Assess just what about that "word," that
moment, might better enable your vision and call. What might be
required, such as licensure or credentials, that could open the doors
in that situation.

My naivete, once accepted to a four-year university, led me to
step into the shortest line in the gym on registration day. A degree
in biology was the result, followed by a college debt of two thousand
dollars. At the time, this amount of debt was frightful and led me
to teach chemistry my first year out. My thoughts had been to pursue a graduate degree in physiology, as offered by another mentor,
Dr. Teunis Vergeer. The hiatus of one year of teaching was simply a
debt-reduction strategy until teaching stole my heart.

Never say no to a God-sized dream, and never miss a moment
of preparation that your life circumstance places in front of you.
Circumstances and certification can be steppingstones to your God-sized dream!

God has called you to something bigger than you can even imagine. Your legacy will be greater than what you can accomplish on earth—your legacy is an eternal and multi-generational Kingdom partnership (think Abraham, Isaac, Jacob and Joseph, each a part of their collective Kingdom assignments). Your uniqueness, your gifts and talents, your passions, circumstances, and your one-of-a-kind relationship with the Holy Spirit will help you navigate how to be the hands and feet of Jesus in the community you're in right now. No preparation is needed in this moment; you are already Kingdom qualified.

Abraham took risks, and he made mistakes. God then provided for him an Isaac to redig his wells, recovering his losses. Jacob, the shrewd one, the conniver in all of us was exhausted, renewed, and only then birthed the dreamer, Joseph. You don't have to see the full journey, just step into your calling, and follow Him!

Go Further

Let's begin your personal handbook:

Do you already have a strong sense of purpose or calling in your life? If so, what is it?

____

____

____

____

If not let me help by asking you to think of a time when you felt fully alive, even if as a child? Describe that moment below.

____

____

____

____

Is there some sense of providence that comes to your mind relative to what you currently are doing in some area of your life?

____

____

____

____

Are there credentials that you feel you are lacking? If so, what are they and how might you pursue them?

____

____

____

____

The womb-work has been done, don't allow your mind to limit your possibilities or your impact on future generations.

CHAPTER 2

Know Your Uniqueness

The true self might be described as our participation in
the divine life manifesting in our uniqueness.
—Thomas Keating

Each person I meet represents a "piece" of God that passes understanding. Bible scholars reading this will have read this as a misquote of Philippians 4:16. In that verse, Paul uses the word "peace." I'll take that risk, given my experience with a Being that is beyond finding out, inexhaustible, and sovereign.

I believe that our Father God assigns a "piece" of Himself to every human born.* It is my belief that your piece, your person, will never be fully replicated or assigned to another. To me, this uniqueness is reflected in the reality of how unlikely it is that you can stand in a mall or high human traffic area and never see the exact replica of any one person.

With each new individual I meet, I experience a previously unknown piece of God. Thus, as I come to know others, I better come to know God. From each person comes a uniqueness, a diversity of thought, a better understanding of the Father, all critical to the Kingdom.

---

* *Pardon the traditional pronoun (himself) being used with this one who sits over trillions of galaxies and far exceeds the bounds of gender!*

You were called from the womb—a fully empowered individual with a piece of God inside you, ever longing for delivery. My hope for you is a revelation of your personal uniqueness. As you become aware of this inner piece, you will begin to understand yourself in new ways; as your personal awareness grows, you will be better equipped to represent your piece of God to the people around you in the marketplace. The more confidence we have in what makes us unique, the greater our representation of the very God in us will be.

There are so many useful personality tests and assessments that can help us better understand how our minds work and what our social and professional proclivities are. Jason Collins, an expert on the Core Values Index, a personality test that measures a person's core values and how they can most contribute to the world, explains the philosophy behind the assessment in an article entitled "Who I Am":

> Who you are at the deepest innate level of your human nature is the most important element in your life. Who you are at this deep level, is, after all, the only thing you really contribute to this world. It is through right assignment and effective choices that you make your highest and best contribution. This is the universal mission of all people. The more you learn about who you really are, and how to optimize your presence in this world, the greater will be your success, happiness and life effectiveness.[1]

The insert above is a more secular way of talking about the piece of God inside each one of us. There really is something at our very core that is unique to us, and when our purpose aligns with it, that is when we are optimizing our presence in the world or bringing the Kingdom of God to earth in a way that only we can. So how do we figure out our piece of God? When we pursue our passions, we can better understand the uniqueness with which God created us, find our giftings, embrace our stories, and practice them in community. By exploring what brings us a sense of fullness and joy, we begin living out the promises of God in ways that attract people and change lives.

Pursue Your Passions

Discovering what your passions are will help you as you work at knowing your uniqueness. What are you drawn to? In life, it's not about finding a job, though at first you may have to work to discover your passion and life's calling. You then simply do what you love, and money will find you. Yes, people will pay to be around you, if you deliver your passion and the skill set that will follow, when nurtured spiritually, academically, and practically. In a nutshell, first find the fun, and the funds will follow.

Think back upon the things you loved to do as a child, dreams you have had that were challenging but inspirational. As a young boy, I was always about setting up clubhouses in old sheds, even constructing tree houses for gathering spaces for neighborhood friends. Perhaps responsible for my later interest in congregations and commercial development? My pursuit of a degree in biology was likely influenced by an uncle, Troy Farmer, who loved the outdoors, hunting, etc. With all due respect, my uncle's impact has likely surpassed many of the professors throughout my "higher" learning to include two advanced degrees.

Answering some of these questions may help you realize some passions that are lying dormant inside your heart.

- What do you lose track of time doing?
- What do you always wish you could be doing?
- What brings you joy and satisfaction?
- What activity makes you feel closer to God?
- What activity helps you feel connected to others?
- When do you feel most productive?

Sometimes passions need to remain as hobbies, but other times our passions can lead us to our Kingdom assignment for the specific season of life we are in. You may already be working in your area of passion; that's great! Reflect on the ways that it brings you fulfillment and satisfaction. How are you using it to serve other people?

Make sure you are capturing your thoughts, be they jotted in the margins or in a separate journal. The whole purpose of this "handbook" is an opportunity for you and God to think out loud as you read.

Find Your Giftings

In order to find your giftings, you have to try new things. And you must be willing not to be particularly good at things at first. For instance, you may have natural people skills. You decide to try your hand at real estate since having good people skills is crucial in that field. This doesn't mean you'll be a real estate prodigy right away; you may struggle with certain aspects because it's new and you're not familiar with it. It doesn't mean you're not gifted or that your gifts don't align, it just means you need to give yourself more time.

Ask people around you what they think your gifts are. This can open your eyes to some areas of your life that you haven't given much thought to. Someone may see potential in you in an area that you had never considered before. Keep your mind open and sit with the answers people give to this question. You may just find something new to try.

While writing this book my mind would often recall moments where comments were made both good and bad about my own giftings or lack thereof. One comment has since marked my mind as an initiator of ideas. That comment was made by my eighth-grade teacher, long before I gave thought to any lofty plans for my life. She timed her comment to the class just perfectly so that I would hear her speaking to a group of "redbirds"; future leaders with whom I had been placed but saw little connection between my giftings and those so evident among those particular students. At that time, I was more comfortable with lower performers with whom I could better compete.

Her statement was, "Why don't you ask Johnny (my given name) his ideas, he always has good ideas." She had previously found a place of esteem in my life such that I recall thinking to myself, "If Mrs. Hill believes that, it must be so!" That tape of her voice has played in my brain for decades and kept me at tables and in board rooms where I might have otherwise shied away from! God, give us more educators like that in our classrooms; she was a model for me during my public-school tenure.

Embrace Your Story

Another element of your uniqueness is your individual story. No one else, not even one of your siblings, has the exact same life story as you. The circumstances in your life, how you reacted to them, the decisions you made, the people you befriended—all of these elements help build your life story.

All of us have parts of our stories that we are ashamed of or wish we could rewrite, but as we talked about in the last chapter, your circumstances, your life-experience often well surpass your certifications in true value. When we embrace our stories and own them for what they are—pathways to redemption—then we are able to reach so many more people with Christ's transformative love. If we are always trying to hide parts of ourselves or our stories, then we aren't fully living out the gospel's impact in our lives. This doesn't mean you need to constantly go around and share all the hairy details of your life story with everyone you pass on the street. It just means when shame is marking part of our identity, it shows up in our words, actions, and interactions. Shame has a way of seeping through to the surface.

Known for her extensive research on shame and resilience, Brené Brown shares in her book *The Gifts of Imperfection*, "Owning our stories and loving ourselves through the process is the bravest thing we'll ever do." Of shame she says, "Shame loves secrecy. When we bury our story, the shame metastasizes."[2] When we try to bury our stories, that's when shame thrives. Think about your life story—where does shame come up? Instead of trying to ignore or bury it, think about how you've overcome that and remind yourself that nothing, no part of you, is beyond Christ's redemption.

We must surrender our story fully to God for transformation and redemption. When we do that, He is able to shine light on the dark parts of our hearts and remove shame so that we can fully embrace our stories and see how they equip us and qualify us uniquely for our Kingdom assignments.

Practicing in Community

Every single person contains a piece of God in them. Our uniqueness is what sets us apart and brings us together as the body of Christ. When you better understand how you were uniquely made and gifted to reflect God to others, you'll be able to live in those giftings more as a way to serve others.

Jesus says in Matthew 25:40, "Truly I tell you, whatever you did for one of the least of these brothers and sisters of mine, you did for me." Jesus teaches us that when we serve our brothers and sisters, we advance His Kingdom on earth. Paul also reminds us that "He who began a good work in you will carry it on to completion" (Philippians 1:6). God has given you special gifts, passions, and abilities that you are able to serve other people with. And when you do, you bring a piece of God to those around you that they haven't experienced before. When we each realize our uniqueness and offer our giftings to the community in this way, we are building up the body of Christ, a powerful ecosystem that works together to create something greater than what any individual part could offer.

Romans 12:4–5 tells us, "Just as each of us has one body with many members, and these members do not all have the same function, so in Christ we, though many, form one body, and each member belongs to all the others." Similarly to this message, Paul states in 1 Corinthians 12:

> Just as a body, though one, has many parts,
> but all its many parts form one body, so it is with
> Christ... Now if the foot should say, "Because I
> am not a hand, I do not belong to the body," it
> would not for that reason stop being part of the

body. And if the ear should say, "Because I am not an eye, I do not belong to the body," it would not for that reason stop being part of the body. If the whole body were an eye, where would the sense of hearing be? If the whole body were an ear, where would the sense of smell be? But in fact God has placed the parts in the body, every one of them, just as he wanted them to be. (1 Corinthians 12:12, 15–18)

We all need each other in the body of Christ. No matter what your profession, passions, or giftings are, you are valuable and needed in the body of Christ. No one part is better than the others; it's not a competition but one, united body. When we are determined to become more aware of our uniqueness, we will realize our unique position within the body of Christ and that will help us as we minister to the people around us and do our jobs in a way that honors God and advances His Kingdom.

Go Further

What value-add can you sense as a possibility as you fully unpack your calling? Write them down as you build your own "handbook" for frequent revisits in the days ahead.

____

____

____

____

Because we each are uniquely qualified, your situation will likely be different. Avoid mimicking what others have done; trust your own "womb work" and uniqueness. Make a list of those traits, gifts, and skills that set you apart?

____

____

____

____

What would divinity look like in you, the divine life "fully" manifest in your uniqueness and within your vocation, your life's calling? How would that change the world around you?

____

____

____

____

Is there a discernable thread or pattern connecting your vocational transitions?

____

____

____

____

CHAPTER 3

Follow Your Gut

*If you're willing to pay attention to and dialogue with what's happening
inside of you, you'll find that your body already knows the answers
about how to live a full, present, connected, and healthy life.*
—Hillary L. McBride, *The Wisdom of Your Body*

Part of building personal awareness is listening to your body. Our
bodies are careful observers and perceivers; our bodies often know
when something is wrong long before we have conscious awareness
of any threat. Many of us view our minds and bodies as separate enti-
ties, but they are more connected than we can imagine. Our bodies
carry helpful intelligence that can help us make decisions, know ourselves better, and live a more integrated and connected life.

A popular teaching within Christianity has been that we cannot
trust ourselves or our bodies (the flesh) and I believe these teachings
have been perpetuated by misinterpretations of Scripture. God gave
us bodies that intricately connect gut, heart, and head, and I believe
this has purpose and value in our lives.

Many people have objections to acting on gut feelings. I've
come to understand a formula that will hopefully help you work
through whatever reservations you may have.

The formula:

1.   Pay attention to your gut feeling;

2. Prayerfully protect the values within your heart;
3. Manage any perceived risks with the third brain located between your ears, but go there only as the last step! Your cerebral hemispheres are most negative, a bias to protect you with flight and fright responses.

Gut, heart, head. Follow your gut, let your heart weigh in, manage risks with your mind. Only when all those elements are involved can we live in the richness of embodiment and intuition.

Gut

We have all heard the expression "gut feeling," but can we really anchor our decisions in what we "feel" in our gut? Your gut is a part of your body, connected strategically to your heart and brain. In a Harvard Business Review Article entitled "How to Stop Overthinking and Start Trusting Your Gut," author Melody Wilding writes:

> Despite popular belief, there's a deep neurological basis for intuition. Scientists call the stomach the "second brain" for a reason. There's a vast neural network of 100 million neurons lining your entire digestive tract. That's more neurons than are found in the spinal cord, which points to the gut's incredible processing abilities.[3]

Our bodies work in tandem with our minds and hearts to give us signals on what decisions to make throughout our days.

On top of the scientific approach to defending the concept of gut feelings, there is also the biblical approach. Your body is the temple of God (1 Corinthians 6:19). Our bodies house the Holy Spirit of God. And God intricately made the body to help us navigate our environments and decisions. In Job 38:36, God asks Job the rhetorical question, "Who has put wisdom in the inward parts or given understanding to the mind?" Our bodies carry wisdom that God uses to speak with us. Irish poet, author, priest, and Hegelian philosopher John O'Donohue puts it this way, "The soul is not simply within the body, hidden somewhere within its recesses. The truth is rather the converse. Your body is in the soul, and the soul suffuses you completely."[4]

At times, following our gut can be much more complex than my simple formula above. In academic terms, it also requires relational and emotional intelligence (EQ), high levels of collaboration, spiritual wisdom, and critical alignment. But like everything, these things come with practice, and I tend to think that approaching things simply is the best route to start with.

In the late 1990s, I had resigned my role at a large church and was truly stepping out on faith, given my family had a new home under construction. In other words, I was becoming a full-blown entrepreneur. That's code language for finding a new way to feed your family! I was wise enough to ask the senior pastor and board not to terminate me until I closed on the home loan.

The journey began with two words that came to me in the middle of the night, Master Counsel. I keep a pad on my nightstand for purposes of capturing ideas. The next morning, I told my wife that I believed it was the name of a company, though I did not know what its mission might be. With the help of an attorney friend, I registered the name and chartered the company. Shortly after that, various people within the community began asking me to serve on their non-profit boards and out of those relationships, opportunities arose to advise other community pastors. I then began to know what the mission of Master Counsel might in fact become.

Soon, I began to transition from my executive pastor role more actively into what initially became a church consulting firm. I anticipated sharing my successes from both my twenty years in education and in ministry. Even though it doesn't make logical sense to begin a company without knowing the purpose behind it, I had a gut feeling that it was the next step for me, and God honored that step of faith. Unexpectedly, I was later asked to contract back with the church I resigned from and served three other senior pastors there for eighteen years.

The Spirit often speaks through gut feelings or intuition—whatever you want to call it. The Creator of life itself has made our bodies so intentionally, purposefully, and intricately, that He uses them as a way to communicate with us about the plans He has for us. That is something we get to be a part of and definitely worth paying attention to.

Heart

The next part of the formula is prayerfully protecting the values within our hearts. The heart is an important part of decision-making processes because it is central to who we are. Proverbs 4:29 tells us, "Above all else, guard your heart, for everything you do flows from it." The old adage now comes to mind that when we wear our hearts on our sleeves, it often leads to hurt because the heart is so essential to our lives and well-being. Our heart guards our values, which are essential to who we are, our purpose, and our motivation. If we do not guard our values or if we hold them loosely, then we are essentially opening ourselves up to destruction and pain.

When you have a gut feeling about something, it's important to let your heart weigh in on the matter. The values at the core of yourself will help you determine if your intuition aligns with those values. Above all, you must protect your heart, so if it doesn't align with a particular opportunity, my advice is to not go down that road. When we know ourselves well, it is easier for us to know when something aligns with our values or not. If we aren't cognitively aware of what we value and what we are willing to stand for, then our lives won't be guided by our values.

Our hearts help us determine the feelings behind our decisions and even during the decision-making process. Emotions carry important information that we should pay attention to as we develop our personal awareness. The more attuned you are to your emotions, the better you'll be able to make wise decisions that align with your gut and values.

Matthew 6:21 tells us, "Where your treasure is, there your heart will be also." When what we value is advancing God's Kingdom through love and faithfulness, our hearts will be aligned with doing Kingdom business. But when our treasure is found in earthly or worldly things, then our hearts will be left unsatisfied and unfulfilled and our decisions will lead us toward a more worldly life. Unless our life has demonstrated a love for others, our success, our wealth, our toys become hollow and meaningless at the end of the day. Figure out where your heart is by looking at what you treasure most.

Mind

Once your intuition and values have weighed in, then—and only then—should you seek the counsel of logic. Your mind is perhaps the most difficult challenge of all. Oftentimes, logic can get in the way of where the Holy Spirit is moving; after all, there is nothing logical about miracles: healings, raising the dead, turning water into wine, etc.

In her book The Wisdom Way of Knowing, Cynthia Bourgeault talks about the mind in relation to spirituality, "In terms of the spiritual journey, trying to find faith with the intellectual center is something like trying to play a violin with a saw: it's simply the wrong tool for the job. This is one reason why all religious traditions have universally insisted that religious life cannot be done with the mind alone; that is the biggest single impediment to spiritual becoming."[5] Our minds, or intellectual centers can sometimes hinder us from walking in wisdom and making the best decisions or from working in the spirit. Unless your mind is both open and disciplined, letting logic weigh in becomes rather difficult.

Of course, our minds are helpful in making decisions every day, and I'm not saying you shouldn't use your mind to make decisions. I'm merely pointing out that culturally, we have elevated the mind before the body and heart as the sole instrument for sound judgment, and I think we should challenge that.

Even allowing God to rewire your mind. Sure, there are disciplines that make the journey less hectic, but periodically and at first daily you will have battles—battles that must be won and some outside the power of the mind and of self-will.

In 2014, I experienced Transient Global Amnesia (TGA), which is an unexplained catch-all for a stroke-like moment that leaves no physical challenges, other than a black hole of less than twenty-four hours. I believe this experience was a bizarre spiritual moment that just happens to fit the definition of the medical terminology referenced as TGA. Peter mentioned something similar in 1 Peter 4:12–13: "Beloved, think it not strange concerning the fiery trial, which is to try you, as though some strange thing happened unto you: But rejoice, in as much as ye are partakers of Christ's sufferings; that, when his glory shall be revealed, ye may be glad also with exceeding joy" (KJV).

The bizarre thing to me has been the nature of my prayers the few months leading up to my TGA experience, that is, that the Lord would somehow rewire my brain. Yes, physically removing the collective damage that comes from the blows of a life fully engaged in passionate Christian service. My prayers asking God to rewire my brain started when I heard a message at church where the visiting speaker referenced a need for the rewiring of our minds, given the long-term toil of life as one matures. As he put it, life may offer a few easy wins, but there are equal times when to win, there seems a need for significant energy output; physically, mentally and at times, spiritually. Those familiar with the spiritual, sometimes categorize these laborious moments as "spiritual warfare." A text often cited is from Matthew 11:12, "the violent take it by force" (KJV).

Yes, there have been moments when the only way through seems to be forceful prayer, even utterances and groanings not understandable to the pray-er. After this man's teaching, I began to pray that God would somehow rewire my mind. Yes indeed, removing the impairments, healing the very synapses that could lead to the offense of others or worse, lessening the impact of my life as an elder. Was this possible? Why not, given that Lazarus was dead for four days, his cerebral matter most certainly near liquid by then! Yet, in the Gospels we read of his conversation at a home gathering shortly after his resurrection. I thought I might be foolish, not to pray toward that end.

My earnest prayers continued for some weeks. Then on a Friday, following a coaching conversation with a friend, I came upstairs from my office, with some apparent symptoms, as later explained by my daughter. Apparently, I kept asking the same questions of a contractor, who was also in the home working on a kitchen renovation. Though I do not recall any of this, I consented to allow my daughter and my wife to take me to a hospital located close to our home in Clemmons. From there, I was immediately rushed to Forsyth Hospital, during which time I strangely recall counting the bridges as the ambulance hurried up I-40 toward the emergency room. The next thing I recall was the annoying sound of the MRI machine.

After seeing multiple neurologists with their typical stroke victim questions: "Mr. Bost, what day is it? When were you born? Who is president?" and three days of numerous tests, they shared the catch-all diagnosis of TGA. Apparently, there are times when one's brain literally resets, typically not more than once in a lifetime. I was later released to shower and go home. As I disrobed from my hospital gown, stepping into the shower for the first time in three days, spellbound by what had happened, I asked the question, "God, what is going on?" Immediately, as by now I am comfortable with the possibility of God speaking, God answered, ***"I've been listening to you pray!"***

In order to fulfill our Kingdom assignments, we need to strive to make decisions with our gut, heart, and mind—all three of our brains. We cannot merely rely on logic to connect with and love the people in our communities well; we need a fully embodied approach to life and business to bring our full uniqueness to the table. Therapist and author Hillary L. McBride writes in her book *The Wisdom of Your Body*, "We do not think ourselves into new ways of living, we live ourselves into new ways of thinking."[6]

Every part of you from your gut to your heart to your mind has important information that will help you navigate situations and decisions. When you take the time to know yourself and listen to what your body is trying to tell you, you will experience more growth and success. Sometimes you may need to ask God to rewire your brain or help you alter your priorities, because logic can sometimes get in the way of the spirit moving in and through us. Start small. What is your gut feeling in this moment? Write that down!

Go Further

Have you had an experience when you followed your gut? What happened? Have you ever ignored your gut feeling? What happened? Be spontaneous with your thoughts from both heart and gut, you can always "adjust your head thoughts" as you read along.

____

____

____

____

Can one really anchor their decision in what they "feel" in their gut?

____

____

____

____

What values in your life and work are most important to you? Note them here. How do you feel when your decisions align with those values? How about when they don't align?

____

____

____

____

How comfortable are you with the idea of letting logic come last in the decision-making process? Ask God to help you trust your gut and engage your heart more as you make decisions this week.

____

____

____

____

CHAPTER 4

Manage Risks and Be Bold

*Now to him who is able to do immeasurably more than all
we ask or imagine, according to his power that is at work
within us, to him be glory in the church and in Christ
Jesus throughout all generations, for ever and ever!*
—The Apostle Paul, Ephesians 3:20–21

One thing that often holds us back from growing in our personal awareness is fear. We fear the risks that are inherent within the journey of self-discovery, namely rejection and failure. As entrepreneurs, we are familiar with risk and many of us probably find a thrill in taking risks. But no one likes rejection and failure. To really know ourselves and grow in self-awareness, we need to learn how to manage risks so that we can live boldly and dream bigger. Managing risks doesn't mean failure and pain won't find you; it just means you are ready for them when they do and you know they won't define you.

God wastes no time nor pain in crafting your Kingdom assignment. Oftentimes, if you listen to people's life stories and testimonies, you'll see God redeem a part of their life that brought them great pain and it will become part of their Kingdom assignment. He doesn't merely take away our pain; He redeems it, fully healing us and enabling us to use our story for His glory. There are times of severe testing, yet deep grace by design, so much so that the very weapon formed to try you cannot defeat you, and in fact, works to your good.

Pause and reflect on a moment of pain in your life that has shaped your very being. It could be a business failure, a loss of relationship, a painful event or experience. How has that experience shaped who you are and how you look at pain, loss, and risk? Most things worth pursuing in life involve risk whether in relationships, business, or elsewhere. When we try to avoid pain and risk at all costs, we end up also avoiding growth, abundance, and joy.

You can't know what your limits and capabilities are if you don't take risks. And even when we take risks that don't align with our capabilities, sometimes that's a great way for us to lean on and trust in God who can do the impossible.

Pain, risk, and losses should be anticipated by any budding entrepreneur. As one mentor shared with me, "Just go ahead and get the first nine failures behind you so that you can focus on the success that often comes with attempt number ten!" Life is full of opportunities to fail, yet without failure, we only increase the probability of later regret. Failing forward is a necessity in life. Learn from others whom you know to be risk-takers. After all, you will soon learn that the objective is risk management, not failure avoidance.

Risk Management vs. Failure Avoidance

Risk management is "the identification, evaluation, and prioritization of risks followed by coordinated and economical application of resources to minimize, monitor, and control the probability or impact of unfortunate events or to maximize the realization of opportunities."[7]

Failure avoidance, in contrast with risk management, involves a dislike of evaluative situations and a fear of failing. It seeks to minimize risk to self-worth in the event of failure, thereby avoiding the negative impact of poor performance in terms of damage to self-worth.

So why should we seek risk management instead of failure avoidance? Because failure avoidance is also growth avoidance. If we're never willing to take a risk for fear of failure, then we are not going to evolve, change, or grow in ways that would be helpful for our lives, businesses, and relationships.

I'm not saying that failure is the objective, nor that we should not take the possibility of failure into consideration. Of course, we should! That's part of risk management. But we can't stop at evaluating the risk of failure; we also need to look at the opportunities for growth and expansion, should failure occur. Would that failure break us or likely, we'd be able to bounce back quickly? If so, that ultimately becomes a WIN!

As entrepreneurs, I'm sure a lot of you have a natural tendency toward risk. You may be thinking that failure avoidance doesn't strike a chord with you at all. But don't tune out so quickly or jump to the next chapter, because the management aspect is an important aspect of all of this. We shouldn't go into decisions blind without looking at information that can help us assess and analyze the possible outcomes. We should look at the facts, look to God, then make a leap.

A research study on failure avoidance showed that "participants preoccupied with the desire to avoid failure had lower self-efficacy regarding their chances to attain specific levels of performance. It seems that failure avoidance makes people prone to judge their own abilities in a less favorable light. In addition, failure avoidance proved deleterious to goal commitment, suggesting that individuals with higher levels of failure avoidance were less inclined to persist in the face of difficulties or to put forth effort to attain a goal."[8] Risk management helps us feel confident, capable, and qualified, while failure avoidance lends itself to catastrophizing, low self-esteem, and negativity.

The way I like to navigate risk management is through 1) assessing risks 2) assessing benefits 3) asking the Holy Spirit for guidance. Anything less is truly risky and can cost you. I learned this lesson the hard way as I began working in commercial development.

Later in my business, given that much of what I was doing with churches was about their expansion, I was advised to secure my real estate license. That soon led to other opportunities particularly related to commercial development. I soon had multiple commercial land tracts under listing, one that had industrial park potential.

While traveling back into town one evening, I noticed a sign advertising a relatively remote tract of land which I knew adjoined my listing. I felt the Lord prompting me to be at the auction, I even called an associate with whom I had worked to join me given his knowledge of the property's potential. The auction required bidders to show proof of funds available at 10 percent of the reserve price set for purchase. I had not thought of purchasing the land, I was merely curious as to who might purchase, so I did not register.

As the bidding began, one gentleman whom I knew kept running the price higher with each bid. He finally came over and asked why I was not bidding, sharing that he was only trying to protect the price of his nearby investment. He by then had the bidding at two-hundred thousand and was maxing out his predetermined exit point. I hesitated at how I would explain this to my wife, but knew I had the means at this point in my new business income stream to acquire the property. The bidding seemed to hesitate momentarily, so I rushed to the folding table set up in the edge of the wooded property for pre-auction registration. The lady rushed as much as she could to secure my information, but the auctioneer was unaware of my intent and suddenly announced, "Sold to the highest bidder!" Once the bid was accepted, the gentleman who now controlled the property, which he had unintentionally purchased, asked that I come by his office immediately after the sale.

I assumed that he would gladly transfer it into my name, having accomplished his purpose of his bidding. However, when we got to his office, a much more seasoned land developer than myself at that point, he asked about my interest in the land. As I naively explained my vision, I could see his wheels turning and I began to realize that my hesitancy and earlier aversion to risk had cost me dearly. He chose to hold the property, assuming our intended plans would bring even more value. I can't tell you how painful it was when I later received a couple calls from those who had left the auction early, assuming that I would be the likely buyer. One offered to buy a portion of the property that had been separated from the main acreage by an interstate at a price near what my immediate out of pocket expense would have been; another inquiring about a long term lease on the remainder!

We are clay in the making, but with choices to be made while actually in the fire. "All things," by God's grace, "do work together for good." But all things are not painless, especially if we come to realize that we could have avoided certain moments, as well as the pain of the moments we missed or failed to maximize. By the way, that auction did introduce me to an agent with whom I was later able to reclaim a piece of environmentally jeopardized land. Without his client's environmental knowledge the land would likely not have been salvageable. That sale paid for my daughter's wedding entirely in 2012 and set up a relationship that soon led to my engagement with a larger development of student housing. One never knows how God might work even your mistakes to your good! That's favor, the beauty of being Kingdom-oriented as an entrepreneur.

Be Bold and Dream Bigger

Ephesians 3:12 tells us that "in him and through faith in him we may approach God with freedom and confidence." On our own, we are not qualified to advance God's Kingdom and make a lasting difference in the world of the eternal, but with God and through our faith in Him, He works in us and through us to build His Kingdom on earth.

Boldness can sometimes be confused with seeking attention or showing off, but that is not how I would define it. Boldness to me means going against the grain for the sake of a higher purpose. You'll see that unfold as you continue to read.

If we look at the life and actions of Jesus, we see that He was bold in His ministry. He didn't mind the status quo or cultural expectations. He spoke truth and practiced kindness. He called out people for injustice done in the name of God. He rebuked people in power, made bold claims, and challenged people's understanding of the laws they'd built their lives around. Jesus is the poster child for living boldly on purpose.

No matter where you are in your entrepreneurial or Christian journey, there are always steps you can take toward living boldly with purpose. Being a Christian in the marketplace will mean that you'll often need to reject the status quo in order to follow your values. You'll have to replace standard business practices with ones that best honor your employees and clients.

Living boldly often means putting others before yourself so that the light of Christ will shine through you. Living boldly will help you grow in your imagination of what's possible with God. Part of assessing risks and living boldly is that it opens you up to dream bigger. When you aren't constantly worried about rejection or failure, your mind will be set free to explore options and dreams that may have been dormant in your heart for some time.

Opportunity is as cyclical as the moon, and seasons do pass, especially moments when collaboration and a greater value-add might have occurred had your gift been brought to the table. With those moments come resources that will better enable the larger Kingdom dream, one that is "exceedingly, abundantly above what you can ask or think" (Ephesians 3:20)!

The great thing about God being able to do infinitely more than you can ask or imagine is that even if you don't achieve what you expected to, you'll still end up with something great and note-worthy. Act on your dreams, test your gut. Sure, hold tight to your heart's values and as best as possible, use those cerebral hemispheres to diminish or manage any risk.

You should always be focused on a bigger dream; one you are somewhat embarrassed to share with any others than the closest of cohorts. Share it anyway! You never know when someone in your circle could have a connection that would help you turn that dream into a reality.

2 Corinthians 5:13–14 says, "If it seems we are crazy, it is to bring glory to God. And if we are in our right minds, it is for your benefit. Either way, Christ's love controls us" (NLT). Take risks and be bold; dream big and let God expand that dream even more. As entrepreneurs with the Kingdom of God in our hearts, God is bound to advance His Kingdom through our skillsets and bring peace and

restoration to each of our communities. You just have to accept the invite.

Through building self-awareness and stepping into your full uniqueness in Christ, you will experience great closeness with your-self and with God. Lean into this closeness and ask God to bring you closer to Him still as you uncover your Kingdom sweet spot. In a meditation adapted from his book *The Universal Christ*, Richard Rohr writes:

> If we can trust and listen to our inner divine image, our whole-making instinct, or our True Self, we will act from our best, largest, kind-est, most inclusive self. There is a deeper voice of God, which we must learn to hear and obey. It will sound like the voice of risk, of trust, of surrender, of soul, of common sense, of destiny, of love, of an intimate stranger, of your deepest self. It will always feel gratuitous, and it is this very freedom that scares us. God never leads by guilt or shame! God leads by loving the soul at ever-deeper levels, not by shaming at superficial levels.[9]

Trust and listen to your inner divine image. It may sound like the voice of risk, but it will lead to a future that you would have thought impossible, a future beyond your wildest imagination.

Go Further

Do you consider yourself a risk taker or do you like to play it safe? Why?

____

____

____

____

What is a big dream on your heart that you're scared to even share with the people closest to you?

____

____

____

____

What is one thing you can do today to boldly declare that you trust God with your life?

____

____

____

____

PART 2

Spiritual Growth

CHAPTER 5

Seek the Kingdom

The seeking of the Kingdom of God is the
chief business of the Christian life.

—Jonathan Edwards

My life has, for many years, been guided by a fascination with science, instilled during my pursuit of what now could be called "a fifth-grade equivalency" of a biology degree from 1970. The degree seeded a need for inquiry that has continued ever since.

In 2020, it was estimated that there were around two trillion galaxies in the observable universe. Each galaxy is unique, ranging in size from ten thousand to hundreds of thousands of light-years wide.[10] Ten thousand light-years would require that one travel ten thousand years at 186,000 miles per second! A width of one light-year is about six trillion miles; it's hard to get my mind around such distances. The light we currently see arrives from those distant sources, yet that very light may only reveal the vestiges of heavenly bodies long ago burned out.

One of my favorite spiritual mentors, Richard Rohr, professes that Christ was first revealed in Creation, secondly in Jesus, and now in the Ecclesia, the body of Christ.[11] When I take that to heart, there are surely as many lessons to learn from Creation as those captured in the sacred texts. Yet Apostle John writes that all the books in his then known world could not contain the full work of Jesus. The mystery and magnitude of the Christ is likely best revealed by the vast heavens with her ever expanding galaxies.

In my early days as a science teacher, I was amazed at how many of the early breakthroughs before and during the Enlightenment Period were linked to the believers. Not all brilliance belonged to the atheistic. Note the following quote from an article entitled "Isaac Newton's Life was One Long Search for God" by Marcelo Gleiser:

> Although we correctly learn in schools that Newtonian physics is a model of pure rationality, we would dishonor Newton's memory if we overlooked the crucial role God plays in his Universe. It may be true that to understand Newton's scientific achievements we can neglect the more metaphysical side of his personality. But that is only half the story—for Newton saw the Universe as a manifestation of the infinite power of God.
>
> It is no exaggeration to say that his life was one long search for God, one long search for communion with the Divine Intelligence, which Newton believed endowed the Universe with the beauty and order manifest in nature. His science was a product of this belief, an expression of his rational mysticism, a bridge between human and Divine.[12]

Though Newton was discovering systems of understanding the earth better, his mind was fixated on things above which are intimately and intricately connected with things on earth. In Colossians 3:1–2 Paul tells us, "Since, then, you have been raised with Christ, set your hearts on things above, where Christ is, seated at the right hand of God. Set your minds on things above, not on earthly things." The idea of heaven is hard to get one's head around theologically, even astronomically given the trillions of galaxies. Setting our minds on things above means seeking and meditating on the Kingdom of

God. When we seek to bring the Kingdom of God to earth, our eyes will be opened to all the ways that God surrounds everything we do.

Spiritual awareness begins by fixing our eyes on things above. When we try to see through the eyes of Christ, we will begin to develop the mind of Christ. As we turn our focus toward spiritual awareness, we'll look at the tools and practices that help us develop a personal relationship with our creator and that assist us on our journey to become catalysts for the Kingdom of God in our communities.

Understanding God's Kingdom

God's Kingdom is a vast concept that has as many interpretations as there are interpreters. Jesus spoke at length about the Kingdom of God while on earth, trying to help people understand a world that is opposite in so many ways to the culture we find ourselves in.

Here are some of the key ways that God's Kingdom is different from our world and more specifically the marketplace:

1. The Kingdom of God is priceless, worth everything you have. It doesn't spoil or fade. (1 Peter 1:4)
2. There will be fewer tears and no pain without gain in God's Kingdom. (Revelation 21:4)
3. In the Kingdom of God, the last shall be first, and the first shall be last (Matthew 19:30)

In our current culture where everything has a price, and often needless pain fills our timelines, where the firsts are rewarded while the lasts are punished, it is hard for us to wrap our minds around a world like the one God promises. The world of the Kingdom is so opposite of what we know and is full of grace, hope, unity, and love. Why wouldn't we want our world to look more like that?

To understand God's Kingdom more, we need to seek to know Him, His heart for His people, the Word He's given us, and His desire for a relationship with us. The more we seek those things, the more Kingdom principles will fill our hearts and minds.

One of the most interesting stories in my early days of transition to self-employment occurred in Mexico while I was on a mission trip. It seems as if the Lord needed me to learn what it really meant to lean on Him for my provision, while remaining aware of those around me in even greater need. I had announced my resignation from the church and was facing both unknown cash flow and little margin for error, the house I was building was completed and we had moved in, but by then were needing a newer car, given that my business would now require more travel.

The morning after we arrived, we were asked to travel to a remote village just outside a garbage dump where people lived, hand to mouth foraging for food and salvaging metal cans, etc., dumped from nearby upscale hotels. We met the missionary serving that village and as usual with a team of mission trippers, he asked that we begin the day with prayer. As we gathered in a circle holding hands, knowing that I had been a pastor, he asked if I would lead the prayer. In return, I asked him how we might pray more specifically. He then near tears, shared that he had just gotten the news that economic hardship would require him to leave his post and return to the states to itinerate for funding unless he could raise $10,000 immediately. Though it sounded like a setup, that was the exact amount of money we had left in savings after closing on our new home. He could not have known that! As I prayed, I ask the Lord what my part might be in this moment. Whether it be my formal training in resource development or my heart for the Kingdom, I found myself both broken for him and strategizing per his need.

Later that evening I asked him to think of donors who had provided large gifts in the past. As a young married man on the mission field, his network was meager. He said his largest donor had given one thousand in the past. I told him to call that person that night and tell him his need, as well that a donor was willing to provide $5,000 of that money if he could match that amount. The next morning, he met me with a smile. Yes, he had his match, and I wrote him a check. So much for the car we needed.

When my wife picked me up at the airport, she said she had a surprise for me. When she opened our new garage door, there sat a like-new four-door sedan, still under factory warranty with only 13,000 miles on the odometer. An acquaintance who knew of my transition, just felt led to provide us with a ride. Ain't that just like God!

Honoring Our Present Home

How can one truly focus on the Kingdom of God without respect for others, an appreciation for the environment, its ecosystems, and given an ever-expanding insight into the galaxies still expect to truly understand the heart of God? Without a demonstrated stewardship driving his or her inquiry, I would also doubt one's ability to hear the Word of God.

That "still small voice" is often heard while taking in the beauty of Creation as well as serving as Christ in places far more stripped of resources than most Americans can appreciate. What if God's full intention for each of us as sons and daughters was indeed "Christ in us the hope of glory"? We occasionally see convincing glimpses in our kindness, charity, and familial love at Christmas, but perhaps our expectations are too low? What if Heaven is here among us, and just as once our full universe was not visible, neither is our full understanding of this destiny we call Heaven?

When we serve our community with our gifts and resources, when we connect people in need with someone who can meet that need, when we uplift the people around us by encouraging them in their gifts, we are bringing the Kingdom of God to earth and in doing so, realizing more of His glory.

How do I balance all this, especially in the context of this polarized republic we call America? Trust me, at times, it's difficult, yet my personal experience with Christ through a radically transformed life at age twenty-five, with both successes and blessings far beyond my preparation, continue to press me further toward inquiry, and with that, daily revelation. Occasionally requiring run-on sentences when I get my praise on! The heavens declare the glory of God, live into that glory.

Keep Your Eyes on the Prize

As entrepreneurs, we have a leg up in this whole Kingdom seeking activity. Our minds are already trained to see a fuller picture of an idea or concept come to fruition. Though the Kingdom may seem far off and intangible as we live out our days on earth, in actuality, bits and pieces of the Kingdom are all around us, and we just have to play our part in bringing God's Kingdom to the earth.

In Hebrews 12:1–3, the author describes our time on earth as a race, "let us run with perseverance the race marked out for us, fixing our eyes on Jesus, the pioneer and perfecter of faith. For the joy set before him he endured the cross, scorning its shame, and sat down at the right hand of the throne of God." As we run this race and continue in our careers as entrepreneurs, let us fix our eyes on the prize, the hope of glory, the author and perfecter of our faith, Jesus. As we keep our eyes on Him, He will build us into who we are meant to be, who we were created to be and we will use our gifts and our piece of Him to continue building the Kingdom on earth as a reflection of what's to come.

As Kingdom catalysts, we are called to grow and deepen our spiritual awareness until we are able to see the world through Jesus' eyes. It's an ongoing, life-long process to seek the Kingdom, but the rewards are eternal and oh so glorious.

Go Further

How do you picture the Kingdom of God? Does it feel far removed or can you see it in your life right now?

____

____

____

____

What actions are you taking to honor your present home? What more can you do?

____

____

____

____

Can you envision a future of a marketplace that looks more like the Kingdom of God? Take some time to think about what that would look like. What would change?

____

____

____

____

CHAPTER 6

Listen to the Spirit

Your call will become clear as your mind is transformed by the reading of Scripture and the internal work of God's Spirit.
—Charles Swindoll

My Bible is now as tethered and torn as this seventy-four-year-old. If you could see her, she is bound together with three-inch-wide strips of Gorilla tape and hard to depart with. Oh, I have other Bibles—versions from years gone by as I have learned the value of early mornings with the text in hand. It's not the stories read repeatedly, nor the closely held doctrines designed by the many religious, that have over the years kept me consistent in my morning ritual. Rather, I have learned to listen to the still small voice that I hear as I read through the words captured by the ancients as they share their journey with God.

But the most beautiful and cherished of moments of my life happens when the Spirit speaks with application fitting for my own journey. That voice sets my heart for the day and deepens the wisdom behind a passionate pursuit of God's Kingdom. I have for years been daily assured of a life impact that will be sustained long after my spirit is released from this body of clay.

To live into your fully unique potential, you need to partner with the Holy Spirit. We can only do so much on our own without the power of God at work within us. However, when our uniqueness is met with the Holy Spirit's guidance, we are able to do way more than we could ever ask or imagine. I hope you will take that as a challenge from the Lord!

Every being understands the concept of an inner voice, self-talk, and conscience. All have heard that voice at some life-threatening moment, or during high-risk decision points when outcomes truly matter. Especially when our accountability is called into question, our spiritual ears become better attuned. Those are also moments where we learn to lean in to hear that inner voice.

The word spirit references your original being, now housed in a fleshly tabernacle, freed only by habitation by the Holy Spirit—that is, rebirth and occupation by the Spirit of God. This invariably results in a new journey toward one's calling and Kingdom assignment.

I think I first learned to listen to God at the age of eleven when I recall, hearing a voice while at play, the words: "One day you will preach the gospel." As I have said before in previous books, I do not recall thinking about God in the moment, praying, or anything spiritual. I was actually playing cowboys and Indians around 1959. I would later experience a vision, awakened from sleep to the sound of orchestra-like music that I had never heard. Once awake, a visual image, virtual but so real that I could touch it sat high above my room as if the sky had come down. It seemed literally a window into the heavens. I now realize how privileged I was as a child. As well, to have a mom who was discerning enough to realize what was happening when I went crying into her room, detailing what was before my eyes. She simply said, "Johnny go back to bed, it's probably the Lord speaking to you." I have always referred to that as my Samuel moment (see 1 Samuel 3:5).

Believers to this day still wrestle with the "unction" of the Spirit. The Kingdom is often held at bay by our hesitancy to act upon what we hear in prayer; and secondly, by our concerns for financial provision on the front end. This can also be compounded by a status quo mentality often unintentionally fostered within our local churches.

All that said, my personal wake-up call only came in January of 1973 with an unanticipated epiphany that my evangelical friends refer to as being born-again. Too much to share right now, but I had unexpectedly walked in on my dad late one night as he was praying for me by name. Again, I am privileged!

The term born-again comes from the Gospel of John and are the recorded words of Jesus. The best lay terms might be that your spirit is awakened, your soul enlightened, and your body energized. Following the direction of the Spirit and becoming attuned to that still, small voice will help you make critical decisions and exude confidence whatever the outcome.

The Counsel of the Holy Spirit

Apart from the counsel of the Holy Spirit, one is left to the mercy of the aforementioned fight or flight wiring—their rational response to fear and risk. Unfortunately, some misinterpret this as self-discipline. The Spirit's journey is far more positive and deliberate than that of FEAR (False Evidence Appearing as Real). There is a better way that affords much more opportunity.

Kingdom entrepreneur and author Shae Bynes wrote about the difference between spirit-guided work and self-sufficient work in her book *Grace Over Grind*. When we fall into the grind mentality, we work from a scarcity mindset, we work because we are afraid if we don't, we will lose everything, or we won't be able to prove our worth to ourselves and others. This is a dangerous mindset to work from. When your work isn't spirit led and led by God's abundant grace, then work will steal your time, joy, and peace. Even when we are "working for God," if we aren't working out of His power and grace, then we aren't working to our full potential and we're not advancing His Kingdom. There is a grace that flows through a "relationship with the Father" as opposed to our sense of need "to work for the Father." The latter is sheer willpower—worse yet, an ill-learned religious fervor!

Working in the spirit means making important business decisions based on grace, prayer, and revelation, rather than fear or selfish ambition. These decisions will lead to greater abundance in every area of your life.

If I go back to the language of self-talk, your inner being or soul sustains an ongoing emotional tension between your spirit and flesh. For those most familiar with Scripture, we are cautioned "to follow the Spirit and not to be controlled by the flesh, with its natural desires." This is a paraphrase from Romans 8; I would invite you to read further for a deeper dive.

Whether serving as an educator, administrator, pastor, business consultant, real estate developer, or even mayor, that still small voice means everything in terms of lasting impact.

Your task is to follow the call, to listen for the voice often while sitting within a felt presence, discerning the circumstances as they emerge. This may occur in a formal worship service or as well be valuable in a boardroom in the marketplace. Stop here and reflect on moments and places where you might have sensed such a presence.

Perhaps we've become confused in our attempts to understand body, soul, and spirit. It would serve us well to learn a language that helps us better think through our theology. The prayerful assistance of the Holy Spirit is necessary especially if we are to exercise and benefit from the Gifts of the Spirit as demonstrated by the Early Church. If a radical transformation does not soon occur within the Institutional Church, along with a renewed sense of power outside of and beyond what well-meaning humans can produce, our influence will continue to diminish.

Unless our theological basis for professing the "Mind of Christ" (Romans 12:2, I Cor. 1:16) is better communicated in a language that culture understands, with some evidence of a spiritual reality, i.e. "signs following," each generation suffers loss and eventually the Church as we have known is left with little value beyond a gathering of folk who think alike, look alike and act alike…we have over 600 local congregations right here in my own community.

My church experience has majority exposure to Pentecostals, though I have consulted with numerous denominations over time. Any reference to Pentecost is however, one that aligns with the book of Acts, guarded as well by a concern for mental health given the emotional tendencies when sovereign power, miracles, and the gifts of the Spirit are in play. That then necessitates the aid of an academically balanced theology, at the risk of over dependence on scholarship, which has unfortunately at times only helped sustain an institutional status quo. That's when one's personal insight, intimacy, faith, in other words, their "soul care" are even more essential, as all these factors help balance the triangle of our spiritual awareness. To practice this balance would likely be transformational for the institutional Church and assure a restored influence within our culture.

Take a moment to struggle with all this before you move on, and I trust you will sense the same urgency as I have felt for years as I have watched the institutional church as I know it, and the manifestation of the Spirit as captured in the canon diminish in its influence within our culture.

Short of just testing God with the ridiculous, learn to trust the Mind of Christ even when cerebral logic pushes back. Sure, you'll make mistakes, just as you have done in your entrepreneurial journey, but that only sharpens your spiritual wit.

As circumstances present themselves, one should prayerfully discern if each misstep might be a "word from the Lord." Not all words are audible. Assess just what about that "word," that moment, might better enable your vision and call.

That "still small voice" is often heard while taking in the beauty of Creation and serving as Christ to our community. Nothing against church, for I have been doing that for fifty years. However, boots on the ground service, whether through your church, your business, or the various non-profits in your community (even holding political office), all provide equal audience with God and man. Don't over spiritualize church attendance such as to minimize lessons learned as you practice your faith in the marketplace. It's all Kingdom stuff!

The process of discernment—learning to hear the voice behind your calling—also requires a deep belief that with that call comes provision, empowerment, and a sovereign landscape within which to work. These are the keys to Kingdom business in my opinion and based upon my life experience.

The Gifts of the Spirit

As a fourth generation Pentecostal, I have seen some amazing things and some things that were clearly "in the flesh" as folk in "the Way" used to say. Amazing healings were commonplace in my earlier life, some just short of raising the dead. I have been "slain in the Spirit" and have participated in moments where others were also as I personally prayed for them. As to the full exercise of the gifts of the spirit, both within and without the sanctuary, I can also attest to.

Why am I sharing all this? It would be paramount to lying if I held back on what I believe to be true for fear of being misunderstood. Yet, being misunderstood can come easily in this relatively new denomination called Pentecostal. I say relatively new, as it had its origin in the Azusa Street Revivals, led by William J. Seymour, an African American preacher. The revival began on April 9, 1906 and continued until roughly 1915. Out of that revival came the Disciples of Christ, The Church of God and the Assemblies of God, all of which I have participated in during my lifetime.

Have they carried forth with the purest of intent the Day of Pentecost, likely no more than others of traditions that today fully deny such practice of the Gifts of the Spirit as Paul outlined. Unfortunately, in our denominational attempts, Pentecostals have emphasized the more emotional of all, speaking in tongues, glossolalia, or one's personal prayer language as the evidence of the infilling of the Holy Spirit. As one who has experienced this gift, as well as interpreted (a whole lifetime cannot explain those moments) I have seen some powerful moves of the Spirit. In fact, one of my deepest experiences occurred in a camp meeting setting, as I found myself speaking French with a stranger, who was originally from France. I only knew that I was speaking in tongues. I say all this for the benefit of Pentecostals that may think that I am belittling their particular denomination when I caution against the emotionally laden practice that occasionally attracts those mentally unbalanced.

One can see how this could go sideways if someone intended to manipulate others, or in some less than humble way held to some sense of superiority among Christians, both motives come from the opposite of being full of the Spirit.

Regardless of the academic expression of ancient doctrines, even from the best of minds, after years of translation from other languages and through numerous cultural shifts, it comes down to one's personal faith, their relationship with Christ and surrender to the Spirit. Trusting in the experiences of others through listening and learning from such experiences is a must, yet much of this journey toward full understanding of one's personal calling comes from listening to the Spirit.

The Confidence of the Holy Spirit

Christianity, especially for an ardent disciple of Scripture, is truly entrepreneurial when it comes to following the Spirit. No pain, no gain; risk and reward; obedience to the Spirit—all are required for high impact.

In order to be trailblazers in our fields and communities, we need to have confidence to go where the spirit leads us to go. We may experience doubt (am I sure this is where the Spirit is leading?), uncertainty (is this really the Holy Spirit speaking to me?), insecurity (why should I be the one to do this?), and fear (what if it doesn't go well?)—this is all normal and doesn't disqualify you from acting in the Spirit. You just have to learn how to quiet all those voices by remembering that God is with you and He works all things together for good. Even if the result isn't what you expected, if you're acting in obedience, then you have nothing to fear.

The more you act in the Spirit and follow where it leads you, the more comfortable you'll become with it. Like anything, practice helps to put you at ease.

In the summer of 1996, I was sitting in a parking lot as I waited for my daughter to apply for a passport for her first mission trip (the same Mexico trip mentioned before). "God," I asked, "where do You want me to be located?" In that same voice that I had now come to recognize, He immediately replied, "Ask Lester for an office." At that time, Lester Burnette managed the former Wachovia Building, now the Winston Tower, which stood directly across from the courthouse where I was parked. Frankly, I was shocked by God's immediate and clear response, and even more, I was hesitant to confront this local businessman whom I had come to admire. I would approach this conversation with great consternation.

The next weekend as I was teaching a Sunday school lesson, I shared the story of the famine in Samaria that took place during Elisha's lifetime. At that time the people of God were surviving off a diet of dove dung and donkey heads. Elisha then prophesied that "tomorrow about this time" a major shift of sorts would occur, to which one of the King's captains responded as if impossible, even if the Lord would open the "windows of heaven." Four lepers, starving outside the gates of the city, determined to take the challenge. "Why sit we here until we die? If we say, We will enter into the city, then the famine is in the city, and we shall die there: and if we sit still here, we die also" (2 Kings 7:3–4). They decided to risk it all and to press into the enemy's camp, even if it meant surrender or, worse yet, death!

Just as I shared that part of the story, I heard the Lord speak to me and even found myself prophesying to the class, "Tomorrow about this time"—looking up at the classroom clock, I noticed it was 10:50 a.m.—"the Lord will open the windows of heaven for someone in this class." That night I wrestled with the Lord concerning that message and what I may have spoken into someone's life. Though it was in the early hours of the morning, I found myself in earnest prayer regarding my calling to the city.

Sometime after daylight, I realized that the Sunday school prophecy may have actually been for me. Was this the beginning of the vision I had seen as a child, that window of heaven? Recalling the Lord's earlier instruction, I called Lester's office sometime after eight on Monday morning, excited about what I thought the Lord was speaking. However, the response from Lester's secretary soon wilted my enthusiasm, "He doesn't even come in on Mondays!" I sheepishly requested that she have him call me if he did come by that day. I then prayed, if this was the Lord, that he would have him call me by the time I had noticed on the clock that day.

Just before eleven o'clock (I would love to say 10:50), my secretary called to inform me that Lester Burnette had just called. I was so excited that I hung up the phone with little instruction and rushed from where I was consulting at the Living Water Family Resource Center to meet with him. When I arrived at his office on the twenty-second floor in the Wachovia Building, his secretary once again informed me that Lester did not come into the office on Mondays and that, in fact, he had notified her of another meeting with someone at a church called First Assembly of God. That was my church, and he was at my office, though his secretary was not aware of it. I then knew God was up to something and hurried to the church, where I found Lester awaiting my arrival. He had simply felt the need to meet with me that day in order to pick up a previous conversation regarding a Christian high school. God is awesome.

Not wasting any of the precious time I might have with this man, I blurted out, "Mr. Burnette, you might think that the cheese has slipped off my cracker, but I believe that God wants me to have an office in your building, preferably on a vacant floor, where I might pray over this city." As I continued talking about my burden to reach our city, struggling to articulate my Joseph-sized dream in a believable way, Lester stopped me long enough to ask, "Will you need a phone?" He was already there. He arranged to meet me in his office the following Thursday.

When I arrived, after being offered some very meaningful advice about my new for-profit company as to how I might approach my dream, Lester took me to a fully glassed corner office on the twenty-fourth floor, which I now believe to be those windows of heaven seen earlier in my vision. There, in an exquisitely furnished executive office, I would spend the next four years praying for a city, two of which were lease free because of Lester's heart for God. The next ten years of my life were spent gaining perspective and watching God answer those prayers.

Go Further

Have you felt the presence of the Holy Spirit in your life before? When was the last time you acted on where the spirit guided you?

____

____

____

____

Historically, what has happened when you've worked in your own strength rather than partnering with God?

____

____

____

____

What roles do doubt and fear play in your business decisions? How can you invite the Holy Spirit into these decisions?

____

____

____

____

CHAPTER 7

Pray for Alignment

Listen to my words, Lord, consider my lament. Hear my cry for help, my King and my God, for to you I pray. In the morning, Lord, you hear my voice; in the morning I lay my requests before you and wait expectantly.
—Psalms 5:1-3

The secret to life is in how you start your day; the rest is about waiting and working with the answers provided, while trusting in the still, small voice. As you grow in spiritual awareness, prayer is an essential tool to walk in sync with God and follow the plans He has for you.

True prayer is conversational intimacy with God. Prayer doesn't change God, it changes us. In fact, at times, prayer turns on me, revealing my weaknesses. But always with that, true prayer provides remedy, insight, strength, and spiritual power. Praying is what helps you align your desires with God's. The spiritual work of personal prayer has honed my ability to hear the voice of God. That, my friend, has made all the difference in my human journey.

Corporate prayer at best affords a sense of my being a part of the whole, the Body of Christ. Mass prayer certainly encourages the pray-ers. However, it sometimes seems Christians believe that numbers move the hand of God. But God has proven over time to be my friend, and friends don't require leverage.

When you're building a relationship with a friend, you need to spend time with them and talk with them often in order to form a deeper relationship. Listening is just as important as sharing in a friendship. Through prayer, you will begin to have continual conversation with God; open your mind and ears to perceive what He's doing in and around you; and receive God's transformation of your desires to align more with His.

Continual Conversation

Do you have that friend that you can go to about anything? If you're having a bad day or saw something weird on the street or you are celebrating a promotion or you're bored, you can just go to them and they'll be there for you no matter what? Those are great friends to have, and we can have that type of friendship with God. Our friendship with God is obviously different than our friendships with fellow human beings. God is perfect and all-knowing; He is our Creator and Father. He is always there for us in ways that the people in our lives can't be.

Learning to pray without ceasing is more art than science. Any art requires time to develop as well as a knowledge of its various media and materials. Eventually keeping an attitude of prayer will become as second nature as breathing.

When we invite Him into these daily moments in our lives we get to experience this type of closeness with Him. When we acknowledge His presence is when we most feel His closeness and love. In 1 Thessalonians 5:16, Paul encourages readers to "pray continually." This might sound excessive to some, but I really think what Paul is talking about here is the type of friendship that is always at our fingertips. Whether we are experiencing something big or small, are trying to make a decision, or need some encouragement, we can always turn to God first with our circumstances and emotions. When we do this, our lives will be marked by more joy, peace, and wisdom.

Open Mind, Open Ears

As we pray, it's important to make sure we're listening to God's response. Imagine a friend calls you because they want to update you on their life, so they update you on everything: how their kids are doing, about their car that needs expensive repairs, what they've been worried about lately and then they just hang up after a ten-minute monologue. You would probably be a little hurt and confused. That's not how friendships work. It's give and take, it's sharing and listening.

When was the last time you waited to hear from God? When you waited patiently for Him to share what is on His heart? Some of you may think that you've never heard from God and that you're not sure that's a real thing. I would like to challenge and encourage you to try listening to Him for a few minutes every day this week. You may not audibly hear from Him; He often speaks to us in creative ways, through a friend, through Scripture, through a memory or picture that comes to mind as we pray. Open your mind to hear from Him in whatever way He wants to communicate with you, then just keep your ears and heart open to receive His message. You'll be glad you did.

As circumstances present themselves, one should prayerfully discern if each might be a "word from the Lord." As an avid reader, I have also become convinced that God often sends books into my life at times appropriate to foster understanding of both my being and the Holy Spirit, now active on the earth. In fact, the last week that I was working on my edits for this manuscript, I received a book entitled, *"Holy Moments"* by Matthew Kelly, affirming much of what I have tried to capture in this book. Perhaps this read will be just such a moment for you!

Listening to God is nuanced and personal. Because you were uniquely made in God's image with a special piece of Him in you, the way He communicates with you and your friendship with Him will be different than anyone else's. There's not a one-size-fits-all when it comes to listening to Him. It's all about learning and growing in your personal relationship with Him.

Transforming Your Desires

In our youths, many of us are prone to think that prayer is about asking God for things. There's even a verse that tells us that He'll give us everything we ask for. But the older I get, the more I realize that prayer is not about getting what you ask for but rather surrendering your will and aligning your heart and desires with God's will.

Jesus shows us what this looks like multiple times throughout the New Testament.

- Lord's prayer: "Thy Kingdom come, thy will be done on earth as it is in heaven"
- Garden prayer: "My Father, if it is possible, may this cup be taken from me. Yet not as I will, but as you will." (Matthew 26:39)
- Last prayer on the cross: "Father, into thy hands I commit my spirit" (Luke 23:46)

In each of these, Jesus surrenders His will for the will of His Father. When we view prayer as a way of aligning our will with God's, then we will begin to see our desires, our outlook, and our thoughts change to become more Kingdom-oriented.

When one fully trusts God, as Dr. Ruth Haley Barton proposes in *Pursuing God's Will Together*, a commitment to "prayers of indifference" is necessary. "Thy will be done" regardless of my desire. Only then will unplanned doors open for your personal calling. I'm talking about doors that the best strategic planning, goal setting, formal preparation, and other business necessities will never open.

As entrepreneurs and as Christ followers, prayer is an essential part of our daily walk. With each initiative comes much prayer; in fact, one learns to pray without ceasing. Often, when people ask me to pray about something, I will say, "Do you think I would be talking with you about this if I were not praying at this very moment!"

Your task is to follow the call, to listen for the voice, often in your quiet time while sitting within a felt presence, or when discerning the circumstances as they emerge. This can certainly occur in a formal worship service, but as well in the boardrooms of the marketplace.

Go Further

Stop right here: 1) inhale, 2) exhale, listen to your body, repeat until you hear
1) Yah 2) Weh, now record your thoughts!

____

____

____

You were designed to call on the name of the Lord, for unceasing prayer! Calling on the name of the Most High, YHWH with each breath opens your heart to the voice. Write down what you are hearing right now!

____

____

____

When I was growing up, people talked about "praying through." For some, it meant praying until another language seized upon your being, glossolalia. For others, it was praying until the prayer manifested as a reality! What has been your experience with prayer?

____

____

____

If the above thought of "praying through" is foreign to you, you might want to talk to a respected spiritual Elder in your community, even outside your own denomination.

Learning to pray without ceasing is more art than science. Any art requires time to develop as well as a knowledge of its various media and materials. Practice prayer!

____

____

____

CHAPTER 8

Study God's Breath and Word

*There are parts of the Bible that inspire, parts that perplex, and parts
that leave you with an open wound. I'm still wrestling, and like
Jacob, I will wrestle until I am blessed. God hasn't let go of me yet.*
—Rachel Held Evans, *Inspired*

I have spent decades reading the text of Scripture; however, the voice
of God, the Word, has been heard more frequently while I am apply-
ing Scripture. Given my experience with the most well-meaning of
theological scholars and clergy, even those to whom the scriptures
were deemed God-breathed were—as we—broken! Yet, no doubt
these broken men and women were used to convey the truths of
God. That's the mystery of the text. What I am saying is the Bible
reveals as much about us and our broken understanding of God as it
does the Word and will of God.

The beauty and mystery of Scripture have guided my life for
decades. Just as gut, heart, and head play a role in achieving your
professional "sweet spot," so do the Scriptures (**God has spoken**) and
the Spirit (**God is speaking**) with respect to the Biblical context and
circumstances, and as you make application per your unique calling,
(**God's Word for you**).

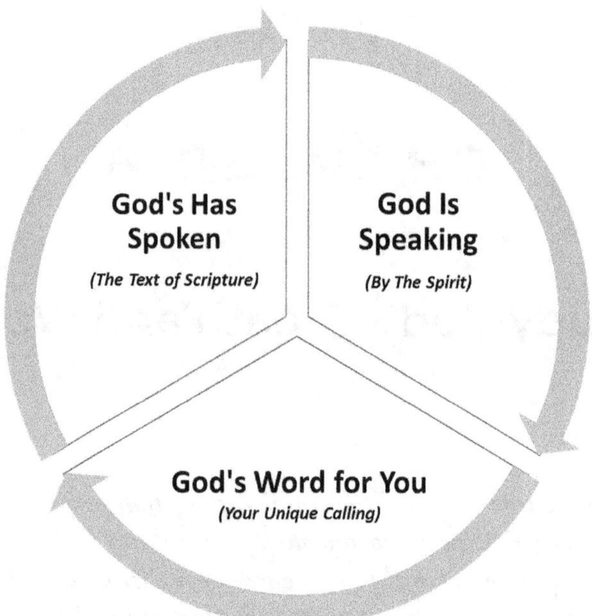

This God-breathed biblical text fully captures the brokenness of mankind as much as the nature of God. Yes, God breathed, but into a brokenness that its writers too often then transferred to God. How else would the nature of Christ have so contrasted with the wrathful God often cast in scriptures? Why do you think the well-intended religious, the elite in terms of formal preparation, misinterpreted both the prophecies and the realities of God becoming flesh in Jesus? So much so that they intentionally killed the Christ.

Not only does the Old Testament capture the brokenness of the best of our biblical heroes, be they Moses, David or Elijah, but even the New provides glimpses of disciples jockeying for position in the Kingdom, Peter vacillating between Judaism and the Way and Paul struggling with John Mark. The good news is that Christ died on our behalf, descended into Hell to set the captives free, then His very body arose, defeating the threat of death—all before his ascension into the heavens, releasing the Spirit of God to dwell richly in our earthly bodies and, with that, a promise that we would do even greater things. There is a lot in that run-on sentence I know! In simple terms, we now have direct connection with the Creator of the galaxies! As the French philosopher Pierre Teilhard de Chardin said, "We are not human beings having a spiritual experience, we are spiritual beings having a human experience."

We make life harder than it was designed to be. We seem to forever struggle with guilt, thus the garden story in Genesis 1. The beauty of scripture is that it actually captures who we are, good, bad, and ugly, while we attempt to understand who God is. God speaks, man writes, and in doing so, too often has transferred that brokenness to God. We then use scripture to reinforce that brokenness in our best attempts at religion. Fortunately, there is Christ, a sure contrast between man's image of God and who God truly is. God is love, it's that simple.

As I age and continue my fifty-year dance with the scriptures, it occurs to me that this holy writ can only be beneficial, if God is breathing in you. Otherwise, the reader is limited to the text and little more than time honored stories about a relationship with God, much of which was limited to the religious bias and understanding of that day.

If God is breathing in you, the text is new every morning, with substantive guidance, even whispers of wisdom heard from within the heart of the reader. Learning to hear the Word while you read the text and then to apply that word to your circumstance is critical to your success and spiritual growth.

Scripture as a Tool

Given my fundamentalist upbringing and evangelical orientation toward the Gospels, you might expect a literalist approach to the Word of God, the text we call the Bible. I must say yes, in a way, but surely one that has morphed over the years since I first began seriously reading the scriptures. You might think it odd, but I was never taught to study the Scriptures as a child, and apart from a religion class in college that required a purchase, I don't recall owning my own Bible. Maybe we could only afford one for the family, as I do remember my parents reading the Bible. It was only when my wife gave me a copy of the Living Bible while we were dating that I started reading it for myself.

Once I had begun attending church as an adult, I was soon asked to teach the adult class in our small church. I assume because I was one of few that held a degree, or the assumption was made that any public-school teacher could surely teach Sunday School. That necessitated my reading and reignited my pursuit of God. I soon came to realize that what I was reading and what I was experiencing in my day-to-day life and its impact on my testimony to others was quite different than the lives of those who wrote these amazing letters. These people were turning their cities upside down!

God breathed into me, and the Spirit's power became so evident, and yet in my earlier readings, without that breath of the Holy Spirit, the words had been mere text on the page, minimally requiring a religious approach to benefit intellectually. Not until I was deep into "the belly of the beast" we call institutional church did I better come to understand an even deeper truth. That is that religion had done a number on us! As the Spirit began to reveal just how much the God-breathed text had also captured the brokenness of religion—first in the Law, the Torah, and then how that brokenness had been transferred to our understanding of the nature of God. So much so that when God showed up in the Christ, just as prophesied and well typified within the sacrifices required, the contrast between law and love was so great that we killed God! You might want to read that again!

It soon became real to my life that the text, though mysterious in its origin and totally improbable, was more tool than Word. John 1:14 tells us, the actual "Word became flesh and dwelt among us" (ESV). Still however, rather than trusting that the Word by the Spirit can use the text, the tool, to speak truth, we memorize the text, using it only as ammunition for doctrinal persuasion, rather than teaching folk to listen to the Word, the Truth, the Christ as we read. Herein lies a great mystery and secret to hearing the call on our lives.

During the editing process, this book even spoke further to me, though I had already spent over a year in its pages. Influenced by what was being spoken to me as I edited, and while reading the scriptures just a few days before finishing I had the Lord speak to me about a verse, which I have likely read over a hundred times. It is found in Hebrews 3:2, but not the one you have likely heard evangelicals emphasize: *"How shall we escape if we neglect so great a salvation..."* No, I was drawn to the second half of that verse: *which at the first began to be spoken by the Lord and was confirmed to us by those who heard Him, God also bearing witness both with signs and wonders, with various miracles, and gifts of the Holy Spirit, according to His own will."*

The writer references a salvation and yes, one the Lord spoke of but one that God bore witness to by way of signs and wonders, various miracles and gifts of the Spirit. When I read the latter part of the scripture, I realized that much of what we offer to others is mere doctrine, confession, and prewritten prayers of repentance, seldom do unbelievers witness situations as described above, with signs following!

The text gave me pause when I think about what all we are missing in a world that is growing more and more skeptical of religion. Sure, reading the text requires a sense for the writer, the context of their day both historical and dispensational. In other words, what was happening in their world, and what God was doing with them at that time in their world. But then one must prayerfully contemplate what the Spirit would be speaking to the reader today in light of the Christ. If Christ is the same yesterday, today, and tomorrow our lives should manifest a similar power and presence of the Spirit as we live and work within our communities, yet our institutions provide little evidence of God's demonstration of the Spirit beyond music, sermons and mere emotion...now I've gone to preach'n!

Assuming a life committed to the Spirit's voice—which best spells out my understanding of revelation—anything less is mere text, religious rigor, and risks the loss of a Word from the Lord that would otherwise lead others to salvation. Ignoring the Spirit while studying the text is dangerous!

How else can one explain the actions of the Pharisees: ultra-religious, well-trained in the law—in fact, lawyers? Yet they were so politically biased by opportunities granted from the privileged in rulership that they missed the very God in Christ that their law foretold. Hmm… Sounds like the peril of today's most religious.

Leaving a Legacy of Revelation

As I read Paul's letters, I have to believe that when he was writing he likely had no idea that thousands of years later his words would be bound together and considered Holy writ. His words would be seen as God's Words, bound in a book whose composite is so rich in story that it is read daily by millions.

That was not likely his vision, but I believe it was God's heart. Had he not labored to get his thoughts recorded for those whom he loved, we would not have this gift of God now treasured by the masses. God breathed; Paul wrote, now the Spirit reveals and empowers.

So much of our spiritual understanding is more wrought than taught, and with time, our beliefs change. Based upon our experience and personal value (if we are open), our boundaries seem ever widening. In my case, much of this has occurred through a disciplined reading of the texts of scripture. Note the use of the words "text of scripture" versus the "Word of God." Reading the text requires an open heart and mind to the Spirit; that voice, once heard, is the Word of God.

If we read scripture simply to be able to recite a few jarring verses, better tell biblical stories or to justify our fixed beliefs, perhaps we are stuck in the same status quo that has now crippled the American church, and likely we have also been disempowered of personal influence, let alone *God also bearing witness both with signs and wonders.*

Spiritual growth is not learning more about Abraham, Jacob, Joseph or Moses. It's about what's happening in me! God forbid that I be stuck in the same spiritual mud of religion that can surround and suck the life from all of us, if we dare not daily seek a new and fresh revelation of the Christ in us!

Go Further

Record a time when God spoke to you through Scripture. How did your relationship with God help you interpret that Scripture?

____

____

____

____

Are you seeking revelation from God daily? What has He been putting on your heart lately?

____

____

____

____

What are you putting in ink so that one day your words will add value to those dear to you?

____

____

____

____

PART 3

Community Development

CHAPTER 9

Build Your Community

Our best intentions are the most impactful when they are formed by the actual needs and desires of our community.
—Dr. David Docusen, *Neighborliness*

Your Kingdom sweet spot will always include loving the people around you in your community and network. As entrepreneurs, having our hand on the pulse of what our communities need is vital to making a difference in our cities. We are called to be the embodiment of Christ, and that means being the embodiment of love.

When Christians think about building community, our minds often go to the people at our church and in our small groups. And yes, that is your community, but it should also expand beyond Church walls.

Kingdom business is about living into one's calling in full community, with each "piece of God" jointly and fully alive. To me, professing communion with Christ apart from a deep and authentic love for one's community and apart from an understanding of responsible stewardship is the antithesis of spiritual wholeness.

If you are thinking that work should be left to the non-profits, I challenge you to consider the following: Capitalism is not a spiritual doctrine, but rather a means of maximizing assets (see appendix), which of course is critical for impact in a cash-based society. Yet our successes should never be used as justification for a bootstrap's philosophy when those to whom we have been called have no boots! With wisdom comes an appreciation for relationship; in fact, one's life over time usually becomes far less self-focused and more "others oriented" with maturity.

As I contemplate the environment within our nation, I can sense a departure from the nature of Christ. With that, a growing loss of true community, even a doubling down attitude regarding our past failures, rather than the confession and redemptive approach once advocated by the Body of Christ.

Over time instead of a natural maturation toward the likeness of Christ, it seems we have chosen exclusivity, self-interest, if not folding into a collective fear of personal loss. In our prosperity, we perhaps have gained the whole world, and meanwhile lost the soul of our nation.

Twentieth century American journalist and social activist Dorothy Day wrote in her autobiography *The Long Loneliness*, "We have all known the long loneliness and we have learned that the only solution is love and that love comes with community." By paying attention to whom is surrounding us, becoming aware of the dangers of isolation, and opening our eyes to others' needs, we can begin to rebuild a community that reflects God's Kingdom.

Question the Box

Recently while reading in Matthew, my mind went back to my first year in Christ. It was in 1973 that I heard Jesus first say, "Follow me." (Matthew 9:9). I recall the newness of life the next morning on January 4 as I drove to the public school where I taught. I think I even cried on the way, mystified by what had happened in my life. Then there were the conversations that week, as I attempted to share with friends this amazing epiphany that had occurred unexpectedly in my dad's living room.

That was awkward, as I had little religious orientation given my near seven-year absence from any true engagement with church folk. All I knew to talk about was science and partying. My fellow teachers and the coaches that I had spent so much time with shooting hoops in the afternoon or at the beach in the summer were beginning to wonder at my life change. Yet like Matthew, I was excited to have them around me, as nothing had changed per my interest in their friendships, I just no longer was the one most likely to leave a party intoxicated.

I guess it was the impact of those who because of their church related activities best understood my life change, and began to engage with me. I even began to feel more comfortable around them, with less doctrinal push back when I was open about what I truly believed had happened in my life. The phrase "born again" seemed most relevant to me, though never with an intent to ostracize others. Eventually, I found myself surrounded by mostly church folk, all very similar in their buy-in to my new lifestyle, in fact I married one. Soon the both of us would become leaders in an interdenominational prayer breakfast and later, after a settling in with an even smaller group, leaders within a single church.

This morning I question that pathway, as the very people that I most enjoyed and was likely called to engage with, soon found me spending the majority of my time with the "saints." My point here is, we humans tend to seek comfort and sameness in our walk with Christ, moreover than simply caring for others, those whose lifestyle may differ. Jesus was not that way! "As Jesus went on from there, he saw a man sitting at the tax collector's booth. "Follow me," he told him, and Matthew got up and followed him.

While Jesus was having dinner at Matthew's house, many tax collectors and sinners came and ate with him and his disciples. When the Pharisees saw this, they asked his disciples, "Why does your teacher eat with tax collectors and sinners?" On hearing this, Jesus said, "It is not the healthy who need a doctor, but the sick. But go and learn what this means: 'I desire mercy, not sacrifice.' For I have not come to call the righteous, but sinners" (Matthew 9:9–12). Scripture always causes me to think outside the box, or at least to question the box I'm in.

Your journey will morph over time as well. Don't be afraid to think outside the box of your particular faith and engage people who have different beliefs than you. Yes, I said what I meant, even among those of different persuasions doctrinally. Iron sharpens iron, be a learner, avoid isolation and siloes; trust the Holy Spirit versus being fearful of delusion by "heretics." Those that promote that fear are often manipulative and controlling. Stay in the scriptures and the Holy Spirit, God's down-payment for His investment in your life (Eph. 1:14) will finish the good work that was begun in you. (Phil.1:6)

It is our responsibility to walk with others, sharing life experiences and where possible, integrating those with lesser spiritual and even financial means into our own journey and our successes. As a Christ-follower, loving others as much as oneself is not an option; it's a requirement. It's a privilege that grace affords. In his book, *Neighborliness*, Dr. David Docusen explores and shares practical ways to cross dividing lines in your community and share love and other resources that your community needs. David writes, "As image-bearers of the same Father, each one of us reflects a different aspect of the beauty of God. When we separate ourselves from others who are different from us, we cannot see the fullness of the beauty of God."[13] When we surround ourselves with like-minded people who do not challenge our faith in any way, we are not actively working to build the Kingdom of God in our cities.

Expand your idea of what community is. Step outside the box that the church can sometimes become and engage with people in your city who need more of the Kingdom of God in their lives.

Danger of Isolation

I recall first introducing computer technology in 1986 during my tenure as a public-school teacher. What a journey it has been transitioning from five-inch floppy disks to thumb drives and now cloud storage.

Of course, I could hardly afford a computer in 1986, having been employed as a teacher for "only" sixteen years. I say that somewhat tongue in cheek, given that teacher salaries are still quite the discussion some fifty years later! I throw that in with hopes that taxpayers and political leaders will eventually circle back to reward these amazing public servants, many of whom have ventured away from the classroom of late, given the complications of COVID.

Fortunately, the technology that we have today has made virtual learning possible, without which even greater damage would have been felt within our schools and community. Technological infrastructure has become a necessity in every home, school, and business community and is vital to market any idea. The good news is the Internet is available to almost anyone—if not in their home, found in any public school or library.

More than ever, folk are finding a comfort level with software and experiencing the freedom of self-employment, fostered by the ability to teamwork from home, connected virtually via Zoom and other platforms. People seem more and more reluctant to go back to a corporate office, emboldened to launch out on their own. With that capability, entrepreneurs are now being raised up every moment of every day.

The other side of that is the growing isolation that has occurred as fewer people share in the impromptu, serendipitous relational moments with coworkers or the pleasant introduction to a stranger during work-related commutes by bus, train, air travel, around the water cooler, or water fountain.

Isolation typically decelerates change, and change drives the market. However, in this COVID age, the unique complexity of the moment seems to have only further challenged the creativity of many and of necessity, opened new doors for ideation. Maybe in these audacious and challenging moments, we are touching upon another Great Awakening? I personally prefer the word transformation, as this moment is not only impacting our churches, but also our schools, work environment and the global supply chain. These are serious moments, yet for the entrepreneur provide great opportunity!

Human interaction is critical for true community, a stabilizer when conflict, even chaos, arises. In moments such as this, humans best reveal themselves spiritually. Unfortunately, we have seen more negativity than inspiration, given the division across our nation. Reduce the impact of congregating, whether in church or civic activities, and adverse circumstance can arise.

Yet these are truly catalytic moments where without spiritual risk-takers, known in ages past as prophetic risk-takers, we are left to the ploy of politicians and power-seekers. Kingdom entrepreneurs have now become even more critical, men and women of ideation that are business savvy, yet driven by selfless love.

As entrepreneurs it can be easy to isolate ourselves to focus on our work, but in doing so, we lose out on the richness of community that comes with personal interaction and alignment with bright minds, those that can encourage and inspire us. As you set out to build a team or even if you already have one, make sure your leadership is others-oriented such that the demands of your workplace do not push people toward isolation.

This age, unlike any we have experienced since early Enlightenment, is complex, and often compounded by archaic remnants of leadership styles framed within the Industrial Age. In *Trust and Inspire: How Truly Great Leaders Unleash Greatness in Others*, Stephen M.R. Covey talks about the dangers of living within an outdated leadership style focused on hierarchies and compliance and introduces a new leadership model for the modern age—one built on trust:

> Command & Control runs along a continuum, represented by two broad categories, though most of the time we don't distinguish between the two. Authoritarian Command & Control operates out of fear: what I can do to you; Enlightened Command & Control operates out of transactional fairness and exchange: what I can do for you (and you for me); by contrast, Trust & Inspire operates out of inspiration and purpose: what I can do with you.[14]

When we are in our Kingdom sweet spot, building trust, inspiring others, and receiving inspiration will naturally occur. You will build a community that thrives.

Grounded in Love

As Americans, we believe that all men and women are created equal and have certain unalienable rights. Surely, then, as Christ-followers, we can leave no one behind. Yet we sit under the shadow of a nation with a growing wealth gap while we religious too often participate in a network of divided houses of worship.

An attitude and action of service keeps our hearts open as we love our neighbors. With service often comes favor, opening doors for business opportunity. Life offers few "either/or" situations for the Christ-follower, but rather "both/and" requirements driven and empowered by love.

Multiple generations living together on this ever-shrinking globe, from late Boomers to Gen Xer's, Millennials and now Gen Z, have provided quite a crucible moment in this now global economy. Sadly, some in earlier generations may have only partially delivered upon their Kingdom calling. That, too, has its Kingdom consequences. So be sure to deliver your piece, fully unpacking your uniqueness.

As we become more relationally aware, specifically focusing on the needs of others in our communities and learning to love our neighbors well, our Kingdom assignments will begin to expand and the impact will deepen. That's when we know we are in our Kingdom sweet spot; when our gifts, the Holy Spirit in us, and our community display the love of Christ unapologetically.

Go Further

How would you describe your current community? Is it homogenous or not? How can you expand your circle some?

____

____

____

____

How can you use the piece of God in you, your uniqueness, to better serve the people in your city?

____

____

____

____

Do your views on capitalism ever interfere with loving others? If yes, how so? If no, how do they support each other?

____

____

____

____

CHAPTER 10

Learn from and Connect with Others

There's no doubt in my mind that what's shaped me and my work more than any particular talent on my part has been living out a calling in the midst of a Christ-centered community.
—Andrew Peterson, *Adorning the Dark*

One is seldom more than six degrees, six "social connections" away from anyone on the globe needed to maximize and market a new idea. This "friend of a friend" web, when trusted, is quite amazing.

A friend of mine in the biotech industry recently shared his experience of burning through millions of dollars in his company's attempts at regenerating human organs. He was near bankruptcy, when one overseas connection made possible by a relationship with the friend of an associate opened the next phase of what will now "save dialysis patients over six hundred billion dollars per year." That particular gentleman, whom he "just happened" to have an audience with, revealed that he had a child with kidney disorders, later writing him a blank check as an investment. The rest is history and happening as I write.

You might say, "I have no offshore connections." God does! The hitch in most folks' gear is that they lack the confidence to continually share their ideas or they fail to deliberately build an ecosystem around them, not yet having learned how to engage connectors appropriately. No one can build God's Kingdom on earth on their own. We need people around us who can help us reach our goals and maximize our gifts.

Assembling Your Team

Seldom do individuals just stumble into success. In my case, it has been about following my gut, sharpening my discernment skills through conversations with both God and others, and then surrounding myself with those who best align with my calling. With each person comes an expanded universe of connections. Learn when and to whom you should share your vision, find ways to interact with those whom you need alignment and relationship. There is power in proximity!

Building an ecosystem of skill sets around you with people that complement your vision is critical. In Malcolm Gladwell's book *The Tipping Point*, he describes three critical players or vital roles with marketing any new concept:

- Mavens, those experts in a particular field or base of knowledge.
- Salespeople, those adept at marketing.
- Connectors, those who can get your ideas and proposals in front of the right people.

With these people on your team, you're now able to work more within your own personal giftings and skill set, thus accomplishing far more than you could on your own. As you develop your relational awareness and begin listening to the Holy Spirit in order to identify people with different skill sets who can help build out your tipping point team, you may even take on a different roles, as you pursue different projects and start additional businesses.

As alluded to in an earlier chapter, the Holy Spirit's voice is not only comprised of auditory sensations, actual sounds, and syllables heard from inside, though unfortunately too often underestimated as mere "self-talk." God speaking can also involve events that transpire in ways often undeniable and beyond our planning. "God moments" sometimes require the unlikely collective action by boards, policy makers, even heretofore known corporate leaders. I am reminded of the window of time when I helped launch Master Counsel Technologies, LLC, in early 2000. I knew little about technology other than my previous days in the classroom, although I had become proficient with both Apple and Microsoft tools.

I had earlier launched my parent company, Master Counsel and Associates, Inc., and under that banner had been coaching a local pastor. He later asked if I might meet with a young man who had just relocated his family to our town. He had moved here believing he was God-sent but was looking for employment. That's a real risk taker!

Upon meeting Robby, I discovered that he was proficient in web design, and I needed a website. Unbeknownst to us, we would experience one of those "six degrees of separation" moments. Robby built my website and did a great job with it. So much so that a former peer had seen Robby listed as webmaster on my new site and invited him to Australia for a consulting gig.

Upon his return, he shared the story of three brilliant "geeks" (I mean that respectfully) who had designed an enterprise level software known as Infra. They were preparing to introduce their new software to the United States. Robby believed it was an opportunity for a new resale firm.

Naively (it's a gift), I asked what might be needed to establish such a firm. He replied, "A team." There were two of us in the room. To me—though I knew little to nothing about the software—two people qualified as a team!

Robby flew to Australia and returned in short order with a certification and license to introduce sales to the USA. We named the new venture, Master Counsel Technologies, LLC (MCT).

I will never forget our first trip as licensed resellers to Cary, North Carolina. Robby was by now well-versed in the technology and had engaged his sister, who was also proficient in a new software tool called *PowerPoint*. As I write, I am feeling ancient given how far all this has come since 2000. We had also paid for one of the three

Aussie founder/designers to attend as an associate. I went along to add bulk.

Upon arrival, we were invited into a corporate boardroom with a professional facilitator and joined by executives flown in from five countries by this multinational corporation. We were given forty-five minutes to present so I sat quietly as Robby and the others shared. He secured our first large contract that day. For ten years, through multiple sales of the software, MCT carried his family of six as Robby practiced his new craft in a global market.

This is only one story of many marketplace examples of God's intervention as two believers decided to follow what seemed in their hearts to be the voice of God within unique and divinely orchestrated circumstances. We later worked together on a lumber startup in Nicaragua, that was one more eye opening experience! When one has seen the hand of God affirming their vision—at times, as personable a journey as walking alongside a friend—let's just say it becomes quite convincing.

Finding your Kingdom sweet spot always involves intersecting with other people and helping them find theirs. When we support one another in our ambitions and gifts, we are better enabling other people to build God's Kingdom on earth, in their own unique way, unpacking that "piece of God" that only they can deliver.

Learn by Listening

Readers are leaders. Again, I have become convinced that God often sends books into my life at times appropriate to foster understanding of both my being and the Holy Spirit, now active on the earth. Reading books is a great way to learn what other Christian entrepreneurs in your field are hearing and doing. Listening to and observing other leaders in your community is another great way to learn from the people around you and increase your relational awareness and capital.

My first introduction to leadership, at least that which I desired to model, was in the Church. I would later study at a graduate level, attempting to make sense of what I saw both in the sanctuary and the marketplace. Still later, I would be attracted equally by those marketplace leaders who bore the image of Christ, as much as the pastors and bishop types I was then serving with. In fact, I saw areas where they could learn from each other in their approach to resolving problems and managing change. That cross-over exchange became my life mission.

I'm a big believer that we can learn something from everyone we meet. And if we carry that attitude and expectation, then we will naturally become better observers, listeners, and learners. Whether it's from books you read, the people on your team, your family, or strangers, get curious and look out for what they have to teach you.

I've often marveled, that the first word of The Rule of St. Benedict isn't "pray," "worship," or even "love." It's "listen." This small, unobtrusive word speaks in a whisper. To anyone who studies Benedictine spirituality, the phrase "listen with the ear of the heart" becomes so familiar we can easily lose sight of how revolutionary it is. Listening in the Benedictine sense is not a passive mission. Benedict (c. 480–547) tells us we must attend to listening. In some translations of The Rule, we are to actively incline ourselves toward it, and nurture it in our everyday activities.

Listening is an act of will. It becomes an easier practice as we wait on God everyday inclining our ear to Him. We have the perfect model of a listener whose ear we have every day. 1 John 5:15 says, "And if we know that he hears us—whatever we ask—we know that we have what we asked of him." As we learn how to listen from Him and how to listen to Him, we will become great listeners for the people around us to share their ideas and step into their sweet spots.

Share Your Ideas

As important as listening to other people's ideas, is sharing your own. Learn to share what you feel you are hearing, seeing, experiencing. Redundancy is a great learning tool so I will say this again, you never know when the person you share the voice with, holds a relationship with some critical player missing from the table, one who could be the key to executing upon your ideation.

Growing in personal, spiritual, and relational awareness will always be an inspiring and idea inducing process. Embrace new ideas for change and progress. Holding yourself static for the sake of the approval of others is to rob yourself of an intimate relationship with the God of the universe. As God works in and through you, share those experiences with others. Even if it feels a little weird or awkward, you never know when it could eternally impact someone's life.

I recall a moment with a former public-school superintendent late one afternoon when he asked for help with a concept which he was toying with to quell a crisis in our district. There was a tense "town hall" meeting that very night. "Don't worry, I have connections!" It felt awkward at first, as it just came out of me and frankly, he was shocked as I was relatively new on the job. I then shared a little further about how important and personal my relationship was with the "Christ in me," the source of my ideation. I recall him hurriedly catching a tear in the corner of his eye. That's hope. We are "prisoners of hope" (Zechariah 9:12). Of course, I then had to produce, so I prayerfully retreated to my office, and surprisingly within about thirty minutes, I had the national leader of that concept on the phone. That night we walked away from that meeting with community leaders ready to launch an educational foundation!

Yes, that's called favor!

Whether you are sharing a new business endeavor, a Scripture that resonated with you, insight that you gained from working on a project, or an idea you have for growing your company, your words and thoughts deserve to be heard. Find people to listen to and find people who will listen to you. This is how we spread good news, hope, and joy.

Go Further

Write down the names of those in your network who come to mind whom you now need to build stronger relationships with?

____

____

____

____

What does your current ecosystem look like? Among your key relation-ships, are there common interests and complimentary skill sets? Are you spending time cultivating relationships and sharing your dreams?

____

____

____

____

Who are some people you actively listen to? How much of your day do you spend listening to others? Pay attention to it this week.

____

____

____

____

CHAPTER 11

Give Generously

*A lack of generosity refuses to acknowledge that
your assets are not really yours, but God's.*
> —Timothy Keller, *Generous Justice*

Relational awareness and community development within entrepreneurship is not just about finding connections who can propel you forward in your business but also becoming aware of how you can give generously to the people in need around you.

As you lead teams and build up your enterprises, you will become aware of the needs of your team, your community, and your city as a whole. To truly find your Kingdom sweet spot, you have to engage those needs and give generously to your people and your city.

The Bible is full of verses about how generosity shows the love of God to those in need and how greed corrupts the soul.

- "It's better to give than to receive" Acts 20:35
- "do not forget to do good and to share with others, for with such sacrifices God is pleased" Hebrews 13:16
- "Whoever is kind to the poor lends to the LORD, and he will reward them for what they have done" Proverbs 19:17
- "If anyone has material possessions and sees a brother or sister in need but has no pity on them, how can the love of God be in that person?" 1 John 3:17

Generosity is near and dear to the heart of God, which means it should be near and dear to us as well, second nature. I strongly believe in capitalism, Christ-centric capitalism. That is, a system that rewards effort and creates means for myself and my fellow man. However, as my ninety-seven-year-old dad, himself raised on a large farm once shared: certain vegetables, if mustard greens qualify as vegetables, must be constantly guarded lest they go to seed! I watched many a time in the garden as he pinched out the tall shoots which otherwise would spend all the plants energy forming mustard seed, while the plant would cease putting on these new and edible, tasteful leaves. Capitalism in America seems to have now gone to seed! As a culture, we seem more about wealth acquisition, than the free practice of one's talents and callings as stewarded gifts from the Almighty, our rewards then appropriately shared with mankind. Capitalism, when bounded by love, has proven itself for centuries.

Let me say upfront, that reasonable investments and an aversion toward debt are necessities for financial wellness. However, for this chapter my focus is about sacrificial sharing, with friends and even at times, relative strangers. One never knows the impact of inner promptings toward simple acts of devotion and love, do them anyway and with generosity. These are the "Holy Moments" I read of earlier in the book that found me!

Faith is an interesting thing to watch when funding is at stake, both personal and corporate—be that environment a church congregation or the marketplace, i.e., business in general. All such sectors are vital and provide opportunity for impact if our uniqueness remains unjaded by the cultural ills that can so easily distract from true community (common unity). Giving that is guided by the spirit, while practicing an abundance mentality, allows us to step into the generosity that Jesus calls us to. That's when one can truthfully preach prosperity!

The Spirit of Giving

"I was young and now I am old, yet I have never seen the righteous forsaken or their children begging bread. They are always generous and lend freely; their children will be blessed." (Psalms 37:25-26). I'm not a hard core "prosperity preacher" but reflecting back on the life I've built with my wife, I can vouch for the scripture you have just read. Our child is blessed, and her children will likewise prosper, as she and her husband pay forward the grace found in generosity.

I can recall choices made during times when generosity held risks for a then young married couple, whether in the form of monetary gifts, loans, automobiles, or furniture. However, I can recall with each moment a clear sense of assurance, followed by the great reward and further reinforcement of felt compassion, true life! Offering our surplus to others who had no financial margin in life, frankly at first felt somewhat illogical, but for the continued prompting of the spirit. Now it is a practice with great purpose.

With resources come responsibility, well beyond the lesser but equally important tithing percentage. A goal for my wife and I has always been to give well beyond the concept of tithing (10 percent). Trust in God surpasses the boundaries of circumstances. He calls us to trust Him in and out of season. Habakkuk 3:17–19 says:

> *Though the fig tree does not bud*
> *and there are no grapes on the vines,*
> *though the olive crop fails*
> *and the fields produce no food,*
> *though there are no sheep in the pen*
> *and no cattle in the stalls,*
> *yet I will rejoice in the Lord,*
> *I will be joyful in God my Savior.*
> *The Sovereign Lord is my strength;*
> *he makes my feet like the feet of a deer,*
> *he enables me to tread on the heights.*

Even when the fig tree does not bud and there are no grapes on the vine, still we should praise God and give of what we have. Just like the widow who gave her two coins which Jesus said was more than anyone else had given.

Toxic Charity

Charity can be toxic when driven by selfish purposes.

Pastor and author Michael Carey writes about toxic charity in his book *Build Hope*:

> "Toxic charity" is generosity that dehumanizes recipients, robbing them of dignity and cultivating dependency. Toxic charity also robs well-resourced people the opportunity to enjoy mutually beneficial relationships with under-resourced people, neighbors who have inherent worth and valuable assets, despite their poverty… Mutually beneficial work partnerships are more enjoyable, yield better outcomes, and are easier to sustain.[15]

On the other hand, true philanthropy is driven by a love for life. Note the root terms *philo* and *trophe*, which mean to love and to nourish. Philanthropy is long-term and strategic, as it often involves making multiple gifts to help the same people over several years. While charity is focused on providing immediate relief to people and is often driven by emotions, philanthropy is focused on helping people and solving their problems over the long-term.[16]

As well, one should avoid any selfish desire to be seen as a do-gooder. That, when coupled with the limitations of IRS deductions, further hampers true philanthropy.

To offer mere charity to those living in poverty (survival at best) while so many of us live in luxury and feel secure within the most coveted country on the globe would hardly seem to rise to the standard of Micah 6:8: "To do justice, love mercy and walk humbly with

God!" For those evangelicals reading, "evangelizing" without integrating others into our own blessings is far less than what either the Prophet Micah or the Christ had in mind.

If I may satisfy my need for graphic illustration (see diagram), please turn your eyes to the right side of the trapezoid and the word "Constitution" which implies governmental assurance as taken from the words of the Declaration of Independence, "unalienable rights" (sic) are to emphasize that everyone is seen by their Creator as having certain rights as protected by our constitution. Our history certainly causes many pause as to whether or not those rights have been fully protected. Though the American Dream is esteemed worldwide, as indicated by the scores who would die to have their children grow up within our borders, we have fallen far short of the redemptive justice and full reparation for the many generations damaged by the misfortunes of our national history.

Capitalism alone does not assure equity, though a Christ-centric community should better provide a broader prosperity. Government (see "law and order") is seldom love based and can neither protect nor tax sufficiently to provide for all those who have fallen through its cracks. Evangelizing was too often the sole objective of church folk as I was growing up, and at times with less integrating of one's converts into their own life successes, rather than the church alone. This fails to fully foster an escape from poverty. Think of the impact of a love based collaborative given the philanthropy poured out across our land. Now contrast that with "Toxic Charity" which more often fosters entitlement, not to speak of scores of competing non-profits, as well as the numerous church plants that dot our cities.

Our task as entrepreneurs desiring to bring the Kingdom of God "to this earth as it is in heaven" (what a mission statement) requires that we integrate others into our personal success, mentoring another generation so as to better assure equal opportunity and a certain learned responsibility. Capitalism works, but only as we understand true generosity and personal calling, sharing in the bounty that a truly moral and love-based capitalism has provided for so many who have known that privilege.

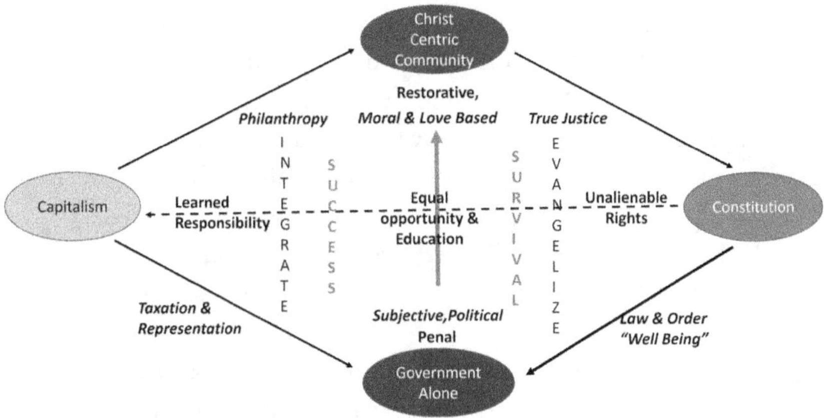

Integrating others, carrying your neighbor along when you find them struggling, sharing your own successes is the very message of the gospel and is how we bring God's Kingdom to earth. Stories like the Good Samaritan were not captured in Scripture only for some pious Sunday moment. We are meant to live out these values.

The current power structures incentivize individual gain and ensure that control is held by a small handful of individuals. The focus is on power over others for short-term profit and fame, rather than shared, equal partnership for long term greater good for everyone. We need to figure out how we can reignite moral and ethical values in this new digital world that will bring us together.

Abundance Mindset

Whether we have an abundance, or a scarcity mindset is a good indicator of our proclivity toward generosity.

The terms abundance and scarcity mindset are often attributed to Stephen Covey, who used them in his book, *The 7 Habits of Highly Effective People*. An abundance mindset is when you believe there are plenty of resources for everyone. A scarcity mindset is when you believe there are limited resources, so if someone else has something, you feel there is less of that resource available for you.

We can be greedy about any of our resources—not just money. We can hoard our time, effort, gifts, and words. If you feel like there's never enough money or time in the day, you probably lean toward a scarcity mindset. But God invites us into a life and a mindset of abundance in Him, "I have come that they may have life, and have it to the full" (John 10:10). To live out this abundance mindset we can be more mindful and grateful of the blessings God has given us, recognizing that at the end of the day, all we have is truly His.

In her book *Braiding Sweetgrass,* botanist and member of the Citizen Potawatomi Nation Robin Wall Kimmerer writes:

> Generosity is simultaneously a moral and a material imperative, especially among people who live close to the land and know its waves of plenty and scarcity. Where the well-being of one is linked to the well-being of all. Wealth among traditional people is measured by having enough to give away. Hoarding the gift, we become constipated with wealth, bloated with possessions, too heavy to join the dance.[17]

Generosity and gratitude help us recenter our hearts on what truly matters. The older I become, the more my mind tends to rehearse the blessings of my life and with a growing gratitude. Yes, once I got my head and heart aligned, I then worked hard at life, learned to look for mentors, following the successes of others who invited me along. However, deep within there is a knowing, even a gnawing that so many of these blessings were sown by others, though reaped by me. I have tried to capture my blessings in a few books, yet my words are never sufficient. The stories are much deeper than the necessity of brevity can provide.

The further back I go in my family's generational walk out of poverty, shouldered upon a deep faith, the more I realize the cost of that journey was paid by so many along the way who, for whatever reason, never knew the benefits in their life which I have known. My hard-working ancestors struggled to capture a piece of the American dream and frankly within their story endured certain moments of unfairness and failure. They got up, brushed themselves off and jumped back into their dream. Yes, being white helped! If that little sting was jarring, you might want to also read Greg Thompson's book, *Reparations: A Christian Call for Repentance and Repair*

In Craig Groeschell's book *Winning the War in Your Mind*, he says, "Money is not and never will be a problem for me. My God is an abundant provider who meets every need. Because I am blessed. I will always be a blessing. I will lead the way with irrational generosity, because I know it's truly more blessed to give than to receive."[18] May we all lead with irrational generosity in a world that is in desperate need of it.

Go Further

When has the Spirit prompted you to be generous? What was the result? If this hasn't happened to you, pray for the Spirit to give you an opportunity.

How would you differentiate charity and philanthropy in your own words? Which one has your giving veered towards?

Do you lean more toward a scarcity mindset or an abundance mindset? Why do you think that is? We can identify differently in different seasons of our lives depending on the circumstances, but we should strive to trust God in and out of season.

CHAPTER 12

Vision for the Future

*Everybody has a vocation to some form of life-work. However,
behind that call (and deeper than any call), everybody has a vocation
to be a person to be fully and deeply human in Christ Jesus.*
—Brennan Manning, *The Wisdom of Tenderness*

Our personal, spiritual, and relational growth will be the biggest
indicators of our success as entrepreneurs. Through the intersection
of each of these areas is how we find our Kingdom sweet spot.

Though our Kingdom assignments may change and our careers
may evolve, our call to be ambassadors for God on earth will not
change and we can continue to rely on Him to lead us to the next
adventure.

As the book comes to a close, I want to encourage you to cast
a vision for yourself of what this growth and Kingdom business
may look like for you over the next few years. God has uniquely
gifted you to serve a purpose on this earth and by seeking Him and
His Kingdom, you can unlock your full potential and creativity. As
Christ-followers, we should possess a creativity that is the envy of this
world and, with that, the ability to provide the very solutions this
world so desperately needs. Creativity seems the sum of three parts:
Imagination, Vision, and Execution.

Your vision for the future should seize you, attract others, and
find its own provision. Otherwise, it is likely mere imagination that

often, when pressed forward, can be personally rewarding, yet of little eternal and Kingdom good!

I can say that the idea of vision has been given a bad rap, even by the church. Often, the term vision is used to announce some theme sufficient to raise funds for one more year of the status quo with few plans to fully execute the changes implied within that vision. I've been on that team also and have a closet full of T-shirts!

I have also come to marvel at the risks taken by secular commercial development teams with whom I have worked. With millions at stake, they press forward from hurdle to hurdle. Yet, at times, their corporate values benefit the greater community in the long term in a way that often surpasses contributions from those professing a Kingdom calling, theirs unfortunately centered primarily on the local church. Remember, I am a church person, so consider this as self-criticism, myself being convicted more as I write!

Having an idea is a good thing. Being seized by vision is another. Vision attracts provision! Vision is the energy that activates the conceptual, bringing capacity beyond one's mind, engaging others, always bigger than self. Full blown realization of ideation, the journey from dream to full execution is quite rare. But when you are pursuing your personal, spiritual, and relational growth, I am of the belief that nothing can stop you from realizing your ideas and dreams, whether you are a pastor, a marketplace entrepreneur or both!

When you work to grow in your personal, spiritual, and relational awareness, you will begin to see the world the way Jesus sees the world and people the way Jesus sees people. Each element of our growth and development is crucial to becoming catalysts for the Kingdom of God on earth. When we know ourselves, know who we are in God and seek Him daily, building up others in our communities and cities, we are fulfilling the mission and calling that God has placed on our lives.

If you want to grow as an entrepreneur and as a Christ follower, you cannot separate the two nor live a compartmentalized life. Everything must be integrated so that you can live the fullest possible life and fulfill the Kingdom assignments God gives you.

I really do believe that the gospel is in the hands of entrepreneurs; that this is a moment of major transformation as we dedicate our time and work in the marketplace to God and for the sake of the people in our community. We don't have to play by the rules or live by the corrupt code of current capitalism; our code is the spirit within us, guiding us and helping us love God and our neighbors with more vigor than ever before.

Think about all the Christ-following entrepreneurs you know. Now dream of a community with all of us living by a different code, a code that takes care of our cities and towns, a code that invites prayer and the Spirit into all our decisions, a code that says "how can we work together?" instead of "what's in it for me?" This kind of gospel living is revolutionary in the marketplace and culture we currently find ourselves in. With the gaps between generations, social classes, employees and employers growing larger each day, the world is in desperate need of entrepreneurs who are dedicated to growing personally, spiritually, and relationally.

As we grow in our relationship with God, we come to a point where we trust Him for the appropriate outcome. Yes, and even to the point of indifference as to how that affects your personal benefit or redirects your vision.

What would our world look like if every Christ-follower approached their occupations with this same passion and vision as most successful politicians, though with the ethics of Jesus? Less hunger, more justice; less sadness, more comfort; less frustration, more fulfilled lives; less war, reconciled nations! Our lives are to be living stones, a demonstration to the next generation of what powerful things the Lord has done in our past. When we step into our Kingdom sweet spot, we magnify our uniqueness for God's glory and pave the way for the next generation of entrepreneurs.

I trust I have laid a pathway toward that spiritual sweet spot that we all seek. And that you have taken the time to listen and capture sufficient word from the Lord in the handbook you personally have now crafted.

Go Further

What is your vision for the future in each of these categories: personally, spiritually, relationally? How are you working toward that vision?

____

____

____

____

Do you view these areas as compartmentalized, or do they feel integrated in your life? How so?

____

____

____

____

How has this book helped you better uncover your sweet spot? What's your next step?

____

____

____

____

Feel free to drop me an email with line or two from the notes captured in your personal handbook: **mastercounsel@gmail.com.**

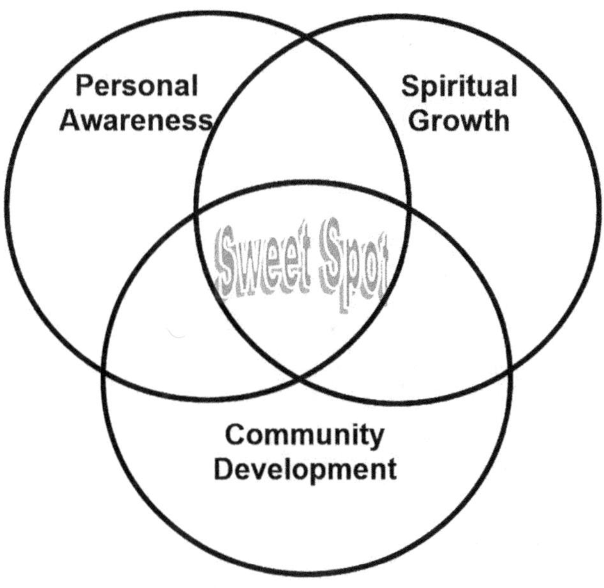

Personal Awareness
Spiritual Growth
Sweet Spot
Community Development

A CLOSING SUMMARY, A PROVERB, AND A PRAYER

In summary, this is how I visualize the unpacking of your "piece" of God, the interconnectedness of the Body and the purpose of each facet of God's plan for each of His children:

God provides
Spiritual capital (a measure of faith)
To enhance your
Human capital (talents, skills, abilities)
To generate and attract
Financial capital
To be stewarded toward
Philanthropic capital
For the sake of
Ministry
Through which we bless others for His glorification and have
Abundant life!

Be not wise in your own eyes; fear the Lord and turn away from evil.
It will be healing to your flesh and refreshment to your bones.
—Proverbs 3:3–8 ESV

This closing prayer was taken from Jim Wallis' book, *Christ in Crisis;* a prayer from a mentor and friend by the name of Mary Glover which was prayed over their volunteer efforts upon passing out bags of groceries *"sufficient to get families through the week, just twenty blocks from the White House."* Think about that!

"Thank you, Lord, for waking me up this morning; that the walls of my room were not the walls of my grave, and my bed was not a cooling board.

Lord, we know that you will be coming through this line today, so Lord, help us to treat you well—help us to treat you well. Amen."[19]

APPENDIX: UNIVERSAL TRUTHS OF KINGDOM WORK

Just days before finishing this book, a friend of mine asked my opinion about a concise statement of processes that are universal in Kingdom work.

Here's an outline of my response to him:

1) Kingdom is flat, no monopolies on calling.
2) Skill sets all sacred, honor that.
3) Listen to those who have done what you desire.
4) Think bigger than what you personally can comprehend or trained to do.
5) Who are those whom God has brought into your ecosystem that can do what you are not called to.
6) Share your vision with those whom you feel would likely push back, learn from the pushback…often those are the ones who will fund the initiative.
7) Don't get ahead of the process required, honor public policies.
8) Don't assume at some point you can now pull it off without those who got you to that point, nor pull in outsiders unless your cohorts agree.
9) Resist ego.
10) Share the celebration, as it's only a beginning.

ACKNOWLEDGEMENTS

Writing a book, in fact a series of books is no easy journey, nor one that is likely taken alone. In my case it has been at the expense of time with family and friends, especially my dear wife, LaDonna. She was the first to hint that one day I might consider writing. Her investment was the purchase of a blank journal presented to me as a birthday gift in 1986. I have been journaling almost weekly since that time. In 2009, I began my digital journal by way of a blog, now in its second iteration, www.johnthecatalyst.com.

As well, my daughter, Summer Elizabeth Jackson and her family have watched my attempts at recording my thoughts now for years from my basement office, thoughts hopefully both spiritually and vocationally attained. The Calling of God is without repentance, in essence it pursues you, assuring your Kingdom piece is fully delivered. As implied in the dedication, I trust that my grandchildren, John Luther and Caroline Elizabeth will also find value in my words as they mature.

No one makes it to the publishing stage without editors, co-writers, colleagues, and authors willing to proof and provide feedback; let alone endorsements, as that is full identity with the writer. In my case, perhaps risky!

During this particular journey, a network formed from within my digital "ecosystem" across the United States. As best as I recall, fellow author, Shae Bynes, Chief Fire Ignitor of the Kingdom Builders Entrepreneur movement based in Florida, and founder of Kingdom Driven, LLC, after reading my previous work, *A Catalyst for Change*, mentioned my name to Jim Baker, now a Senior Pastor in Ohio with whom I had worked. She then tracked me down by way of a fellow Floridian and author, Dr. David Docusen, who most recently published, *Neighborliness* just before moving to my hometown. After about nine months of conversation, it would be Shae's recommendation that I consider a developmental editor, Tori Thacher from Washington State. Tori had assisted Shae in one of her books, *Grace Over Grind*.

As well, it was my dear friend, Michele Bryant Powell, author of "*15 Minutes of Unpacking Our Grief,*" whom I have served alongside of both she and her late husband, Stephen Powell for almost three decades, who recommended Covenant Books as my publisher. Ashley Matthews of Covenant has been quite patient given my numerous iterations of this manuscript.

Above all, to God be the glory!

OTHER BOOKS

John has now authored four other books, all available on Amazon.com:

1. Most recently, *The Christ I Came to Know: Pulling Out of Poverty and the Parallels with Relearning Religion.*
2. Another, a coauthored look at one man's journey of service in five community sectors, by John Bost and Patty Sawvell: *A Catalyst for Change: How Alignment and Relationship Accelerate Change.*
3. One now most prophetic booklet from 2009: *Repo: The Church in Foreclosure.*
4. One children's book, *Jake and John*, illustrated by Rebecca Hodson.

All available on Amazon or at my website:
www.JohnTheCatalyst.com

ENDNOTES

1   Vos & Howden, LLC. "Core Values Index." eRep. Accessed January 20, 2023. https://erep.com/core-values-index/sample-innovator/?mode=full.

2   Brené Brown. *The Gifts of Imperfection*. New York: Random House, 2020.

3   Melody Wilding. "How to Stop Overthinking and Start Trusting Your Gut." Harvard Business Review, March 11, 2022. https://hbr.org/2022/03/how-to-stop-overthinking-and-start-trusting-your-gut#:~:text=The%20Science%20Behind%20Your%20Gut,lining%20your%20entire%20digestive%20tract.

4   "Daily Meditation: Embodied Wisdom: Weekly Summary." Center for Action and Contemplation, August 13, 2022. https://cac.org/daily-meditations/embodied-wisdom-weekly-summary-2022-08-13/.

5   Cynthia Bourgeault. *The Wisdom Way of Knowing: Reclaiming an Ancient Tradition to Awaken the Heart*. San Francisco, CA: Jossey-Bass, 2003, 31.

6   Hillary L. McBride. *The Wisdom of Your Body: Finding Healing, Wholeness, and Connection through Embodied Living*. Toronto, Ontario, Canada: Collins, 2021.

7   "Risk Management." Wikipedia. Wikimedia Foundation, January 10, 2023. https://en.wikipedia.org/wiki/Risk_management.

8   "Failure Avoidance Motivation in a Goal-Setting Situation—Researchgate." Accessed January 20, 2023. https://www.researchgate.net/publication/233136250_Failure_Avoidance_Motivation_in_a_Goal-Setting_Situation.

9   "Daily Meditation: Listening to the Voice of God." Center for Action and Contemplation, July 20, 2022. https://cac.org/daily-meditations/listening-to-the-voice-of-god-2022-07-29/.

10 "How Many Galaxies Are There in the Universe?: Amount & Discovery." The Nine Planets. Accessed January 20, 2023. https://nineplanets.org/questions/how-many-galaxies-are-there-in-the-universe/.

11 "The First Incarnation." Center for Action and Contemplation, February 16, 2019. https://cac.org/daily-meditations/the-first-incarnation-2019-02-21/.

12 Marcelo Gleiser. "Isaac Newton's Life Was One Long Search for God." Big Think, April 4, 2022. https://bigthink.com/13-8/isaac-newton-search-god/.

13 David Docusen. *Neighborliness: Love like Jesus. Cross Dividing Lines. Transform Your Community*. Nashville, TN: W Publishing Group, an imprint of Thomas Nelson, 2022.

14 Stephen M. R. Covey. *Trust and Inspire: How Truly Great Leaders Unleash Greatness in Others*. New York City, NY: Simon & Schuster, 2022.

[15] Michael Carey. *Build Hope: 40 Days with Nehemiah to Bless Your World*, 2022.

[16] "Philanthropy, Volunteerism, and Charity—Rutgers University." Accessed January 20, 2023. https://njaes.rutgers.edu/money/pdfs/lesson-plans/DoE-Lesson-Plan-21-Philanthropy-Volunteerism-and-Charity.pdf.

[17] Robin Wall Kimmerer. *Braiding Sweetgrass*. Vancouver, B.C.: Langara College, 2022.

[18] Groeschel, Craig. *Winning the War in Your Mind: Change Your Thinking, Change Your Life*. Grand Rapids, MI: Zondervan Books, 2021.

[19] Wallis, Jim, and Michael B. Curry. *Christ in Crisis: Why We Need to Reclaim Jesus*. HarperLuxe, an imprint of HarperCollinsPublishers, 2019.

ABOUT THE AUTHOR

John Bost served twenty years in the public school system, both in the classroom and in administration. He holds two post graduate degrees, one in community development and the other in Leadership and Administration. A bi-vocational minister for almost 50 years, he served eight years as a full-time executive pastor in a large growing congregation. A former chair of Leadership Winston-Salem and a three-term mayor for the Village of Clemmons, he would later serve two terms as chair of the Shallowford Community Foundation and be named as their first board member emeritus. John is currently active in an ongoing commitment to racial reconciliation and educational equity in Forsyth County.

He is married to LaDonna Setzer Bost, a retired educator and interior designer. They have one daughter, Summer Bost Jackson, now in her sixth year as a public-school principal. His son-in-law, Chris Jackson, is on staff at Wake Forest University; he has two grandchildren, John Luther and Caroline Jackson.